CLASSIC
DISHES
Made Easy

CLASSIC DISHES
Made Easy

Mechthild Piepenbrock and
C. P. Fischer

Hamlyn
London · New York · Sydney · Toronto

English edition published by
The Hamlyn Publishing Group Limited
London · New York · Sydney · Toronto
Astronaut House, Feltham, Middlesex, England

First published under the title
Die schönsten Rezepte leicht gemacht
© Gräfe und Unzer GmbH, Munchen 1982

ISBN 0 600 32335 8

Photography by C. P. Fischer
Front cover photograph by Robert Golden

Phototypeset by Tameside Filmsetting Limited in 9½ pt Monophoto Times
Printed in Italy

Contents

Useful Facts and Figures

Notes on metrication

In this book quantities are given in metric and Imperial measures. Exact conversion from Imperial to metric measures does not usually give very convenient working quantities and so the metric measures have been rounded off into units of 25 grams. The table below shows the recommended equivalents.

Ounces	Approx g to nearest whole figure	Recommended conversion to nearest unit of 25
1	28	25
2	57	50
3	85	75
4	113	100
5	142	150
6	170	175
7	198	200
8	227	225
9	255	250
10	283	275
11	312	300
12	340	350
13	368	375
14	396	400
15	425	425
16 (1 lb)	454	450
17	482	475
18	510	500
19	539	550
20 ($1\frac{1}{4}$ lb)	567	575

Note: When converting quantities over 20 oz first add the appropriate figures in the centre column, then adjust to the nearest unit of 25. As a general guide, 1 kg (1000 g) equals 2.2 lb or about 2 lb 3 oz. This method of conversion gives good results in nearly all cases, although in certain pastry and cake recipes a more accurate conversion is necessary to produce a balanced recipe.

Liquid measures The millilitre has been used in this book and the following table gives a few examples.

Imperial	Approx ml to nearest whole figure	Recommended ml
$\frac{1}{4}$ pint	142	150 ml
$\frac{1}{2}$ pint	283	300 ml
$\frac{3}{4}$ pint	425	450 ml
1 pint	567	600 ml
$1\frac{1}{2}$ pints	851	900 ml
$1\frac{3}{4}$ pints	992	1000 ml (1 litre)

Spoon measures All spoon measures given in this book are level unless otherwise stated.

Can sizes At present, cans are marked with the exact (usually to the nearest whole number) metric equivalent of the Imperial weight of the contents, so we have followed this practice when giving can sizes.

Oven temperatures

The table below gives recommended equivalents.

	°C	°F	Gas Mark
Very cool	110	225	$\frac{1}{4}$
	120	250	$\frac{1}{2}$
Cool	140	275	1
	150	300	2
Moderate	160	325	3
	180	350	4
Moderately hot	190	375	5
	200	400	6
Hot	220	425	7
	230	450	8
Very hot	240	475	9

Notes for Australian users

In Australia metric measures are now used in conjunction with the standard 250-ml measuring cup. It is important to remember that the Australian tablespoon differs from the British tablespoon; the table below gives a comparison. The British standard tablespoon, which has been used throughout this book, holds 17.7 ml and the Australian 20 ml. A teaspoon holds approximately 5 ml in both countries.

British	Australian
1 teaspoon	1 teaspoon
1 tablespoon	1 tablespoon
2 tablespoons	2 tablespoons
$3\frac{1}{2}$ tablespoons	3 tablespoons
4 tablespoons	$3\frac{1}{2}$ tablespoons

NOTE:**When making any of the recipes in this book, only follow one set of measures as they are not interchangeable.**

Introduction

The choice of recipes in this new and original illustrated cookery book is not a chance selection nor does it simply reflect our own personal taste and judgement. We selected the dishes by giving a collection of famous, well-tried and, at the same time, exciting recipes to a number of cooks – beginners, experts, amateurs and professionals – and asking them to choose those which they felt were indispensable for a book such as we envisaged.

We laid great emphasis on the word 'selection', for we were both of the opinion that quality was more important than quantity. The result is a colourful mixture of well-loved international specialities including many different types of recipe – sophisticated dishes, subtle dishes, country dishes and simple dishes – among which we are sure you will find many new favourites.

The book is unusual because the recipes are very detailed. We thought it extremely important to describe the method in such a way that even a beginner has a good chance of success. Each recipe was worked out, tested, cooked and photographed without embellishments, and because the book was written for all those who enjoy experimenting with new recipes but do not perhaps have the courage to attempt Pike Quenelles in Cream and Basil Sauce, Liver Pâté or the supposedly difficult Charlotte Royale, the text and pictures were designed so that the cook can see at a glance whether the result is like that in the photograph.

We tried to describe all the difficult stages in the recipes very clearly both in words and pictures: for instance, making a soufflé, beating a custard over hot water or simply poaching eggs. 'Know how' is just as important in cookery as in any other job and so the simple but necessary steps such as peeling and deseeding tomatoes, preparing peppers and chopping onions are described in exact detail for, if you are not familiar with the techniques, you need far more time for preparation and often fall short of complete success.

The book has been arranged in the classical manner: soups and stews, salads, vegetable dishes and starters, eggs, fish, meat (veal, beef, pork and lamb), poultry and game and desserts.

Ambitious amateur cooks who enjoy presenting their guests with a succession of well-balanced dishes will find many suitable ones in this book. There are also a good many recipes for those who do not wish to spend too much, as well as a wide choice of sumptuous meals, hearty country-style dishes, celebration dinners and simple light suppers.

What is offered here is much more than just a collection of superb photographs of delicious-looking food. The detailed instructions will give you the confidence you need to prepare and serve every single recipe as if you were a master in the art of cookery. You will certainly decide that cooking some of the world's classic dishes was never so easy or so much fun.

We hope that leafing through these pages and cooking the recipes will give you much pleasure and that you and your family and friends will share our enthusiasm for these classic dishes, for it was enthusiasm which prompted us to write this book.

Mechthild Piepenbrock
C. P. Fischer

**Unless otherwise stated, all recipes
are for 4 persons.**

Barcelonessa Soup

Herbs, garlic, lemon and tomatoes give the tasty Barcelonessa soup its typically fresh character. It is served with spicily seasoned meatballs and garnished with fresh parsley and chervil.

---

450 g/1 lb piece of lamb
(shoulder, breast or leg)
1.5 litres/2¾ pints cold water
1 bunch fresh parsley · 1 small leek
1 stick celery · 1 onion
2 cloves · 1 bay leaf
1 sprig fresh thyme · salt
freshly ground black pepper
2 cloves garlic
150 g/5 oz lean minced lamb
1 egg · cayenne pepper
3 tablespoons plain flour
2 ripe tomatoes
3 tablespoons fine fresh breadcrumbs
15 g/½ oz butter
1 teaspoon tomato purée
4–5 tablespoons olive oil
1 teaspoon lemon juice
1 handful fresh chervil leaves

Preparation time: 2–2½ hours

Rinse the lamb under cold running water and place in a large saucepan with the cold water. Bring to the boil slowly, skimming off any grey scum as it rises to the surface. Meanwhile take one sprig of the parsley, rinse it under cold running water and shake dry. Trim the leek and celery. Rinse leek well to remove grit. Chop both vegetables and the sprig of parsley coarsely.

Peel the onion and press the cloves into the surface. Make a slit in one side of the onion with a sharp knife and insert the bay leaf. Rinse two more sprigs of parsley and the thyme and shake dry. Place them in the stock together with the chopped vegetables and onion. Season with salt and pepper. Reduce the heat until the liquid is just simmering and cook gently, partially covered, for 1½–2 hours. The stock should never be allowed to boil.

Just before the stock is ready, prepare the meatballs. Peel and chop one clove of garlic. Rinse and dry half the remaining parsley and chop it finely. Place the minced lamb, garlic, chopped parsley and egg in a bowl and mix together thoroughly, seasoning generously with salt, pepper and a little cayenne pepper. Form into small balls about the size of a walnut.

Roll the meatballs in the flour to coat on all sides. Leave for a few minutes to allow the flour to dry on the surface.

Scald the tomatoes in boiling water for 10 seconds, then peel and remove the core and any pieces of hard stem. Cut in half so that all seed chambers are visible and, taking half a tomato at a time in the palm of your hand, squeeze gently until seeds fall out. Discard the seeds, and chop the tomatoes finely. Peel and crush the second clove of garlic and mix with the breadcrumbs. Melt the butter in a frying pan and fry the breadcrumbs until they are golden brown.

Remove the meat from the stock and reserve it for use at another time. Strain the stock and return to the saucepan. Skim as much fat as possible from the surface of the stock and bring to the boil again. Add the tomatoes and tomato purée and stir vigorously. When the stock returns to the boil, stir in the fried breadcrumbs which act as a thickening agent. Reduce the heat and simmer, stirring frequently, for 5 minutes.

Meanwhile, heat the oil in a frying pan over high heat. Add the meatballs and fry briskly until browned on all sides and cooked through. Shake the pan constantly as you are doing so to prevent the meatballs from sticking to the pan. This should take about 5 minutes.

Season the soup with salt, pepper, cayenne pepper and lemon juice, then add the meatballs. Chop the chervil and remaining parsley finely. Serve the soup piping hot, sprinkled with the herbs.

1 **Preparing the onion.** Press the cloves into the onion. Make a slit in one side of the onion with a sharp knife and press the bay leaf firmly into it.

2 **Rolling the meatballs in flour.** Place the flour in a shallow dish and roll the meatballs carefully in it. Put them aside for a few moments to allow the flour to dry.

3 **Thickening the soup.** Stir the fried breadcrumbs and garlic mixture into the boiling stock. Reduce the heat and simmer for 5 minutes, stirring frequently.

Our tip

As with all soups, the quality of the stock is of decisive importance for the flavour and consistency of Barcelonessa. The meat, with or without bone, is first placed in cold water and brought to the boil extremely slowly. During this process a layer of thick grey scum will form on the surface. This must be skimmed off frequently until the stock clears or until the foam becomes fine and white in appearance. During the whole cooking process the stock must not be allowed to boil otherwise the scum will not settle on the surface and, as a result, the stock will not be clear. Should the stock begin to boil, add a little cold water so that the temperature drops below boiling point. The scum should then slowly rise to the surface again.

Prawn Bisque

The preparation of Prawn Bisque requires a good deal of time, but it is well worth the effort. Virtually no other soup tastes so exquisitely delicious.

16 Dublin Bay prawns or scampi, fresh or cooked, each weighing about 50 g/2 oz
1 bunch fresh dill
6 litres/10 pints water
50 g/2 oz salt
2 carrots
2 shallots
1 small onion
2 sprigs fresh thyme
3 sprigs fresh parsley
75 g/3 oz butter
4 tablespoons brandy
600 ml/1 pint dry white wine
1 bay leaf
25 g/1 oz plain flour
450 ml/¾ pint single cream
freshly ground white pepper
cayenne pepper

Preparation time: 2½ hours
Cooling time: about 2 hours

If you have been able to obtain fresh, uncooked prawns, scrub them thoroughly under cold running water. Rinse the dill and put a little aside for use as a garnish later. Put the rest of the dill in a very large saucepan with the water and salt and bring to the boil. Boil for 5 minutes so that the pan is thoroughly hot; the addition of the prawns should not reduce the water temperature. Add the prawns to the fiercely boiling water and continue to boil for 1 minute, then reduce the heat and simmer for a further 5 minutes. Remove the pan from the heat and put aside to allow the prawns and stock to cool. This will take about 2 hours.

Peel the carrots, shallots and onion and chop very finely. Rinse the thyme and parsley under cold running water, shake dry and chop coarsely.

Remove the prawns from the stock and twist off the tails. Pick the meat from the tail shells and remove the intestinal cord. This looks like a black thread and is found on the back of the tail meat. It can be easily removed with a sharp knife. Put the shells on one side together with the legs which should also be removed. Break open the claws by twisting the smaller half of each at the joint and cracking open the larger half. Remove the meat without separating the two halves of the claw. Put aside a few of the better claws and a few whole pieces of tail meat to use as a garnish. Pound the rest of the meat to a fine paste and put aside.

Divide the shells into portions and pound each portion in a mortar with a pestle, or grind to a pulp in a blender or food processor, adding a little stock if necessary. Heat 40 g/1½ oz of the butter in a heavy frying pan. Add the vegetables, herbs and crushed shell. Heat, stirring occasionally, until the mixture begins to take on colour. Add the warmed brandy and ignite. Let it burn for a few seconds before quenching the flames with half of the wine. Add the bay leaf and cook for a further 10 minutes, then pass the mixture through a fine sieve.

Melt 25 g/1 oz of the butter in a saucepan. Stir in the flour until it has been absorbed then add the rest of the wine, the sieved shell purée and the prawn meat paste. Stir in the cream and cook for 5–10 minutes or until the liquid has reduced a little and acquired a creamy consistency.

Remove the pan from the heat. Cut the remaining butter into small pieces and whisk them into the soup. Season to taste with salt, pepper and cayenne pepper and serve immediately, garnished with the few whole pieces of prawn meat and claws that were set aside and the rest of the dill.

1 **Cooking the prawns.** If dealing with live prawns, grip each firmly by the back and place head first in the boiling water, pressing it immediately under the surface.

2 **Removing the meat.** Twist off the tails and pick the meat from the shells. Remove the intestinal cord, the black thread found on the back of the tail meat.

3 **Breaking open the claws.** Twist the smaller half of the claw at the joint and break open the larger half. Remove the meat so that the two claws halves are not separated.

4 **Pounding the shells.** Reduce the shells to a pulp in small portions using a mortar and pestle, or a blender or food processor. Heat 40 g/1½ oz of the butter in a heavy frying pan and add the vegetables.

Our tip

The shells must be thoroughly pounded in order to release their full aroma; for this you can use a pestle and mortar or a blender or food processor. Whatever is used, the job will be made easier if the shells are first broken or crushed with a cleaver or large kitchen knife.

Paella

Paella could be best described as a 'Spanish stew' for that is basically what it is – meat, fish, vegetables, rice and spices cooked together in one pan. Some of the ingredients may vary according to the season.

450 g/1 lb fresh mussels
6 tablespoons dry white wine or water
150 g/5 oz French beans
salt
8 large prawns, fresh or frozen
(about 350 g/12 oz)
1 small oven-ready chicken (800 g/1¾ lb)
150 g/5 oz pork fillet · 2 onions
3–4 cloves garlic · 1 red pepper
2 large ripe tomatoes
6–8 tablespoons olive oil
freshly ground black pepper
300 g/11 oz rice
900 ml/1½ pints boiling water
½ teaspoon saffron powder
225 g/8 oz chorizo sausage
100 g/4 oz frozen peas
8 stuffed green olives
lemon quarters to garnish (optional)

Preparation time: 1½ hours

Scrub and clean the mussel shells thoroughly in several changes of cold water; discard any which are already open. Remove the beards. Cook the mussels in the wine or water in a large wide pan for 5 minutes, then remove from the shells. Discard any mussels which have not opened. Strain the stock.

Trim the beans and break into 2.5-cm/1-in lengths. Part-cook them in boiling salted water for 3–4 minutes, then drain in a colander and refresh under cold running water. If using frozen prawns, thaw them first and pat dry with kitchen paper. Divide the chicken into eight pieces, wipe the pieces with a damp cloth and pat dry. Cut the pork into 1-cm/½-in cubes. Peel and chop the onions and garlic. Halve the red pepper, remove the core and seeds, and cut into strips about 5 mm/¼ in wide. Scald the tomatoes in boiling water for 10 seconds, then peel, remove the core and discard the seeds. Chop the flesh finely.

Set the oven at moderately hot (200°C, 400°F, gas 6). Heat 3 tablespoons of the oil in a paella pan or shallow flameproof casserole. Season the chicken pieces with salt and pepper, add to the pan and brown them well on all sides. Remove the chicken and fry the prawns for a few minutes. Remove the prawns and discard the oil. Heat the remaining oil (3–5 tablespoons) in the pan until it is hot. Brown the pork cubes and remove, then fry the onions, garlic and red pepper gently until they are soft. Add the chopped tomatoes and cook briskly until the juices in the pan have been substantially reduced.

Rinse the rice in a sieve, shake dry and place in the pan with the vegetables. Cook for a few minutes, stirring well, before adding the boiling water and the reserved mussel stock. When the rice becomes translucent, season with salt, pepper and saffron and bring to the boil, stirring constantly. Remove from the heat.

Slice the chorizo and place in the pan together with the chicken pieces, pork cubes, prawns and beans. Stir the frozen peas under the other ingredients; they should be completely covered with liquid. Place the pan in the heated oven and cook for about 30 minutes or until the rice is tender. Stir in the sliced olives and the mussels 5 minutes before the end of cooking. Serve immediately, garnished with lemon quarters if desired.

Our tip

Do as the Spaniards do and cook the paella over an open wood or charcoal fire at your next barbecue. Follow the recipe but increase the amount of liquid – more will evaporate when it is prepared in the open. Stir the paella frequently during the cooking process so that the ingredients cook evenly and the rice on the surface does not become hard and dry. Paella is traditionally served straight out of the pan, with a fresh salad of tomatoes, mild onions and lettuce handed separately. Spanish wine goes best with paella, of course, although chilled lager makes an acceptable alternative.

1 **Adding the tomatoes.** Add the chopped tomatoes to the vegetables in the pan and, stirring briskly, cook over a fierce heat in order to reduce any liquid from the vegetables.

2 **Seasoning the rice.** Season the rice with salt, pepper and saffron when it has become glassy in appearance. Bring to the boil, stirring constantly, then remove from the heat.

3 **Adding the peas.** Make sure that the frozen peas are well covered with liquid otherwise they will dry out during the cooking process. Place in the heated oven and complete the cooking.

Chilli con Carne

Very hot, very sharp and very substantial – that is how Chilli con Carne, the fiery Mexican stew, should be. It is just the thing to serve at an informal party. If you cannot get the beans mentioned in the recipe, you can of course use other dried beans (white, brown or black). Do not, however, add the salt or the tomatoes earlier than mentioned in the recipe since both prolong the cooking time of beans.

Serves 12

---

800 g/1¾ lb dried red kidney beans
800 g/1¾ lb dried pinto beans
6 litres/10 pints water
8 onions
6–7 cloves garlic
2 kg/4½ lb lean topside of beef
6 tablespoons olive oil
4–5 chillis (fresh or dried)
3–4 sprigs fresh oregano
3–4 sprigs fresh thyme
2 sprigs fresh sage
2 tablespoons sweet paprika
½ teaspoon cayenne pepper
1.5 kg/3 lb tomatoes
salt
freshly ground black pepper

Soaking time: 12–24 hours
Preparation time: 2½ hours

Rinse and drain the beans. Place them in a large saucepan with the cold water and leave them to soak overnight. On the following day, bring the soaking water and beans quickly to the boil. Continue to cook over a moderate heat for 30 minutes.

Peel the onions and chop them finely. Peel and chop the garlic. Wipe the meat and cut into 2-cm/¾-in cubes. Heat about half of the oil in a large, heavy-based saucepan and fry the meat, a few pieces at a time, until it is well browned on all sides. Remove each portion as it is browned and place in a metal sieve with a dish underneath to catch any juices. Add more oil to the pan if necessary. As soon as all the meat has been browned, heat the oil in the pan once more and place all the meat in it, without the meat juices. Cook, turning, for a few more minutes until really brown and crisp.

Push the meat to one side of the pan and fry the onions, stirring frequently, until they are soft and golden. Then add the garlic and cook for 2–3 minutes, taking care that it does not burn. Add the beans and the liquid in which they were cooked. One can do this by carefully pouring them from one pan into the other or by using a large ladle. The ladle method avoids the dangers of splashes of hot liquid and steam.

Cut open the chillis and remove the seeds. Rinse, pat dry and cut them across into rings. Dried chillis should be lightly crumbled. Rinse the herbs and shake dry. Place in the stew with the chillis. Season with paprika and cayenne pepper. Add the meat juices, cover the pan and simmer gently for 1 hour.

Meanwhile scald the tomatoes in boiling water for 10 seconds, then peel and remove core and any hard green stem. Cut tomatoes in half so all seed chambers are visible and, taking half a tomato at a time in the palm of your hand, squeeze gently until the seeds fall out. Discard these, chop the flesh coarsely and add to the stew with salt to taste. Cook for a further 15 minutes, then season to taste with pepper and more cayenne pepper if liked. Serve very hot.

1 **Chopping the onions.** Cut the onions in half lengthways. Slice each half parallel to the work surface. Then slice lengthways vertically and then across into even dice.

2 **Frying the onions.** Push the meat to one side of the pan and, stirring frequently, cook the onions until they are soft and golden. Then add the garlic.

3 **Adding the beans.** Pour the beans and the liquid directly from one pan into the other, or transfer them with a ladle to avoid danger of splashes of hot liquid.

Clam Chowder

In the United States this creamy shell fish soup is usually served with unsalted crackers.

---

1 kg/2 lb fresh mussels
1 kg/2 lb fresh or bottled clams
2 onions · 2 carrots
2 sticks celery, or ¼ celeriac
2 bunches fresh parsley
6 tablespoons dry white wine
salt
freshly ground white pepper
75 g/3 oz smoked streaky bacon
2 small green peppers
350 g/12 oz potatoes
2 sprigs fresh thyme
2 large ripe tomatoes
1 tablespoon butter or oil
1 tablespoon flour
6 tablespoons hot chicken stock
6 tablespoons hot milk
150 ml/¼ pint single cream
pinch sweet paprika
1 sprig fresh dill

Preparation time: 1 hour

Scrub and clean the fresh shell fish thoroughly in several changes of cold water. Discard any which are already open. Remove the beards by holding firmly between thumb and knife blade and scraping off. Place the shell fish in a large pan.

Peel and finely chop the onions and carrots. Trim the celery and slice, or peel and dice the celeriac. Put half the bunch of parsley aside and coarsely chop the remainder.

Put the carrots, celery or celeriac, half the onions and the chopped parsley in the pan with the shell fish. Pour in the wine and sufficient water so that the shell fish are just covered. Add a little salt and a generous amount of pepper. Cover the pan and quickly bring to the boil. Shake the pan frequently so that all the shell fish get an equal amount of heat. Boil for about 5 minutes or until all the shells have opened. Remove the shell fish and discard any which are still shut. Strain the stock through a paper coffee filter or through a fine sieve lined with a damp cloth. Set aside.

Trim any rind from the bacon and chop finely. Halve the green peppers, remove the seeds and core, and cut into fine dice. Peel and dice the potatoes. Rinse the thyme and shake dry. Put aside one sprig of the remaining parsley and chop the rest finely with the thyme. Scald the tomatoes in boiling water for 10 seconds, then peel and remove the core and any pieces of hard stem. Cut the tomatoes in half and, taking half a tomato in the palm of your hand, squeeze gently until seeds fall out. Discard these and chop the flesh.

Fry the bacon gently in a large pan until the fat begins to run. Add the butter or oil and fry the remaining onion and the green peppers until they are soft. Sprinkle the flour over the ingredients in the pan, stir in and cook until it becomes golden and frothy. Mix together the chicken stock, shell fish stock and milk and add to the pan, stirring constantly. Bring to the boil, stirring. Add the potatoes, chopped herbs and tomatoes and simmer for 15 minutes. Stir in the cream and simmer until the liquid has reduced and the soup has acquired a creamy consistency.

Remove the mussels and clams from their shells (or drain bottled clams) and chop about three-quarters of them. Place the chopped and whole shell fish in the soup and heat through gently. Season with paprika and garnish with the dill and reserved parsley sprig before serving.

1 **Straining the stock.** In order to remove any sand, strain the stock through a paper coffee filter or through a fine sieve lined with a damp cloth.

2 **Adding the flour.** When the bacon, onions and green peppers are soft, sprinkle the flour over them and stir until the liquid becomes golden and frothy.

3 **Adding the liquid.** Mix the shell fish stock with the chicken stock and the milk and pour slowly over the vegetables, stirring all the time until it comes to the boil.

Our tip

The best times for fresh shell fish are the months with an 'r' in them – September to April – and shell fish should be alive when purchased. Discard any which are not tightly shut or do not shut immediately when given a sharp tap. Shell fish which are open are usually dead and therefore poisonous. The same rule applies to shell fish that do not open during the cooking process: they should also be discarded. You can prepare clam chowder with canned or bottled shell fish as clams are not often available fresh. However, it is essential to use clams in brine as shell fish preserved in a marinade are too strong in flavour.

Ratatouille with Lamb

This combination of lamb, vegetables and fresh herbs stewed together in their own juices produces a beautifully aromatic dish.

2 large ripe tomatoes
2 cloves garlic
2 onions
1 red pepper
1 green pepper
2 small aubergines
2 medium-sized courgettes
$\frac{1}{2}$ small leek
1–2 sticks celery
450 g/1 lb lean boneless lamb
(from the leg)
6 tablespoons olive oil
salt
freshly ground black pepper
2 sprigs fresh rosemary
2 sprigs fresh thyme
1 bunch fresh parsley
1 bunch fresh basil
1 bay leaf

Preparation time: 1$\frac{1}{2}$ hours

Scald the tomatoes in boiling water for 10 seconds, then remove the skins and any hard pieces of core. Cut the tomatoes in half so that all the seed chambers are visible and, taking half a tomato at a time in the palm of your hand, squeeze gently until the seeds fall out. Discard the seeds.

Peel the garlic and onions. Chop the garlic finely and slice the onions. Halve the red and green peppers, remove the core and seeds and chop into fairly large pieces. Rinse and dry the aubergines and courgettes. Remove the stalks and cut into halves or quarters lengthways, then slice crossways. Trim the leek and celery and slice both thinly. Place the leek in a sieve and rinse to remove any soil that might remain. Wipe the meat and cut into 2-cm/$\frac{3}{4}$-in cubes.

Set the oven at moderately hot (200°C, 400°F, gas 6). Heat the oil in a wide flameproof casserole and brown the meat, a few pieces at a time. When each portion is well browned, remove from the pan and place in a metal sieve with a dish underneath to catch the meat juices. When all the meat is browned, add the onions to the casserole and fry in the same fat until softened. Remove the onions with a slotted spoon and continue frying the vegetables, one after the other: first the peppers, then the aubergines, the courgettes and finally, the leek and celery with the garlic.

Put all the fried vegetables back in the casserole with the meat and add the tomatoes and the meat juices. Season to taste with salt and pepper. Rinse the herbs and shake dry. Set half the basil aside and chop the rest of the herbs finely. Stir into the ingredients in the casserole and place the bay leaf on top. Cover the casserole and place it in the heated oven. Cook for 45 minutes. Taste and adjust the seasoning, discard the bay leaf and serve garnished with the rest of the basil.

Our tip

In Provence, Ratatouille is more often served without meat as a vegetable stew, and it makes a refreshingly light and tasty summer or autumn dish which can be served hot or cold. If served cold, it must be seasoned again before serving as the intensity of the seasoning diminishes during the cooling process. Composed entirely of vegetables, Ratatouille makes an excellent accompaniment for grilled or fried meat or can be served cold as a starter. Cold Ratatoille can be garnished with basil as well.

1 **Removing the seeds from the tomatoes.** Cut the tomatoes in half so that all the seed chambers are visible. Squeeze gently so that the seeds fall out, and discard the seeds.

2 **Cut the meat into small cubes.** Heat the oil in a flameproof casserole and brown the cubes of meat well, adding them in batches to avoid crowding the pan.

3 **Mix the meat with the vegetables** and pour the meat juices back into the casserole with the tomatoes. Season with salt and pepper to taste, add the herbs and continue cooking in the oven.

German Beef and Vegetable Soup

This unusual variation on the theme of vegetable soup, with generous amounts of beef and herbs and a bacon and mushroom garnish, shows that it does not have to be a boring and unimaginative dish.

---

1 bacon bone
450 g/1 lb stewing or
braising steak
2 litres/3½ pints water
1 bay leaf
4 carrots
½ celeriac
1 leek
1 bunch fresh parsley
2 sprigs fresh marjoram
2 leaves fresh lovage (optional)
800 g/1¾ lb potatoes
salt
freshly ground black pepper
grated nutmeg
6 spring onions
100 g/4 oz mushrooms
100 g/4 oz smoked streaky bacon

Preparation time: 2 hours

Wipe the bacon bone and the beef. Place the bone in a large saucepan with the water and bring slowly to the boil. When the stock is boiling, add the beef and the bay leaf and return to the boil. Skim off any grey scum which rises to the surface. It will be necessary to skim a number of times. Partially cover the pan and simmer gently for 1¼ hours. Check occasionally to see if any more scum has accumulated on the surface and skim off. While the stock is simmering, prepare the vegetables.

Peel or scrape the carrots and cut into neat dice. Pluck any leaves from the celeriac, rinse and shake dry. Peel the celeriac and chop into neat dice. Trim the leek and slice into 5-mm/¼-in rings. Place in a sieve and rinse to remove any soil which might remain. Rinse the herbs, shake dry and chop finely together with the celeriac leaves, if any. Peel the potatoes and cut into 1-cm/½-in cubes.

Place the vegetables in the stock and season to taste with salt, pepper and nutmeg. Continue to simmer for a further 30 minutes. Just before the end of cooking time, trim the spring onions. Cut the white part of the onions into small dice and the green stalks into neat rings. Clean the mushrooms and slice as thinly as possible. Remove the rind from the streaky bacon and cut into tiny cubes. Fry the bacon gently in a frying pan until the fat runs out. Add the spring onions and fry, stirring occasionally, until golden. Add the mushrooms and fry briefly. Drain the mixture on kitchen paper and set aside.

Remove the beef and bone from the soup. Discard the bone. Place the beef in a sieve so that any stock runs off. Remove any fat or gristle and cut the beef into neat pieces.

Remove about one-third of the vegetables from the soup and place in a dish. Mash these vegetables with a fork and put back into the soup together with the beef. The mashed vegetables give the soup a thicker consistency. Stir the soup well to distribute the beef. Taste and adjust the seasoning, and discard the bay leaf. Add the bacon and mushroom mixture and serve immediately.

1 **Preparing the carrots.** Peel or scrape the carrots and trim off the ends, then cut lengthways into strips of equal size and finally into small cubes, using a sharp knife.

2 **Dicing the potatoes.** Peel the potatoes. Cut into slices 1 cm/½ in thick. Lay the slices on top of one another, cut into strips and then across into dice.

3 **Preparing the meat.** Place the cooked beef in a sieve to drain off any stock, then carefully remove any fat or gristle and cut the meat into neat pieces.

Our tip

If you cannot obtain a bacon bone, double the quantity of beef and include a beef bone. Add a thick piece of bacon rind to the stock to enhance the flavour.

Bigos

Bigos is a Polish national dish: a hunter's stew. Cook it slowly so that the flavours of the various meats and vegetables blend well together.

---

225 g/8 oz beef topside
225 g/8 oz lean stewing veal
225 g/8 oz lean boneless pork
225 g/8 oz boneless venison
(from the shoulder)
150 g/5 oz garlic sausage,
in one piece
100 g/4 oz mushrooms
½ small white cabbage
(about 350 g/12 oz)
1 apple
2 onions
150 g/5 oz tomatoes
25 g/1 oz butter
1 (312-g/11-oz) can sauerkraut
2 tablespoons oil
5 tablespoons Madeira or
white wine
250 ml/8 fl oz chicken or
beef stock
1–2 sprigs fresh marjoram
2 cloves garlic
pinch cumin seeds
2 whole allspice
1 bay leaf
salt
freshly ground black pepper

Preparation time: 2 hours

Wipe all the meats with a damp cloth. Cut into 2.5-cm/1-in cubes, keeping each kind of meat separate. Roughly chop the garlic sausage. Clean the mushrooms and halve any large ones. Remove dry coarse outer leaves from the cabbage. Cut the cabbage in half, remove the core, rinse, drain and shred finely. Peel and core the apple, slice thinly lengthways and then once crossways. Peel and chop the onions. Scald the tomatoes in boiling water for 10 seconds and peel. Remove core and any hard stem. Cut tomatoes in half so that all seed chambers are visible and, taking half a tomato at a time in the palm of your hand, squeeze gently until seeds fall out. Discard, and chop the flesh coarsely.

Set the oven at moderately hot (200°C, 400°F, gas 6). Melt half the butter in a flameproof casserole and fry the apple and onions until lightly browned, turning frequently. Drain the sauerkraut, if liked, and break it up with a fork. Place in the casserole together with the mushrooms, cabbage and tomatoes. Continue to cook over a moderate heat for 5 minutes, stirring occasionally, then remove from the heat and set aside.

Heat a little of the oil and remaining butter in a frying pan. Fry each kind of meat separately, finishing with the pieces of sausage, until well browned on all sides. Add more oil and butter with each batch. As soon as each batch of meat is browned, place it in the casserole on top of the vegetables so that any meat juices run over the vegetables. When all the meat is in the casserole, mix the vegetables and the meat together.

Heat any fat or juices remaining in the frying pan and add the wine and stock. Bring to the boil, stirring constantly with a wooden spoon to loosen any sediment sticking to the pan. Boil to reduce the liquid.

Meanwhile rinse and shake dry the marjoram. Tear the leaves into small pieces. Peel and chop the garlic. Add the marjoram, garlic, cumin seeds, allspice and bay leaf to the casserole and season to taste with salt and pepper. Gradually pour the reduced liquid over the meat and vegetables, shaking the casserole from time to time so that the liquid is well distributed. Cover the casserole and place in the heated oven. Cook for 1½ hours or until all the meats are tender. Taste and adjust the seasoning, and discard the bay leaf before serving.

1 **Placing the meat on the vegetables.** Place each batch of browned meat on top of the vegetables as soon as it is done so that any meat juices blend with the vegetables.

2 **Removing the meat sediments.** Heat the fat again and add the wine and stock. Stir to loosen any sediment and then boil to reduce the liquid.

3 **Adding the liquid.** Pour the mixture of wine, stock and meat juices over the vegetables slowly, so that the liquid becomes well distributed.

Borsch

Whether you serve Borsch as a main dish or as a little snack during an informal party (in which case this recipe will be enough for six), this hearty beetroot soup based on the Russian original will always find enthusiastic takers. Serve it with wholemeal bread and chilled lager.

---

800 g/1¾ lb lean beef brisket
2 small marrow bones
2.5 litres/4½ pints water
3 onions · 4 carrots
1 leek · 1 stick celery
5–6 sprigs fresh parsley
2 bay leaves
450 g/1 lb fresh beetroot,
uncooked
½ celeriac · 2 cloves garlic
40 g/1½ oz butter
½ teaspoon sugar
4 tablespoons red wine vinegar
½ small cabbage
225 g/8 oz tomatoes
salt · 100 g/4 oz cooked ham
2 frankfurter sausages
freshly ground black pepper
5–6 sprigs fresh dill
150 ml/¼ pint soured cream

Preparation time: 3½ hours

Wipe the beef and the bones and place in a large saucepan. Add the cold water and bring to the boil over a gentle heat. Reduce the heat and remove any grey scum which has risen to the surface with a skimming spoon. This must be done several times to produce a clear stock. The stock should now simmer very gently; never allow it to boil or the scum will not rise and settle. If the stock should begin to boil, add a little cold water to reduce the temperature.

Meanwhile, peel two of the onions and two of the carrots. Trim and wash the leek and celery. Coarsely chop these vegetables. Rinse the parsley, shake dry and chop. Place the vegetables, parsley and bay leaves in the stock and turn up the heat to bring it back to simmering point. When the stock begins to simmer, reduce the heat a little, partially cover the pan and cook very gently for a further 1 hour.

Remove the beef and place on one side. Continue to simmer the stock and vegetables for a further 1 hour. The pan should only be partially covered so that the stock gradually reduces to about 1 litre/1¾ pints. At the end of the cooking time, strain the stock and remove as much fat as possible.

Peel and chop the remaining onion. Peel or scrape remaining carrots, the beetroot and celeriac and cut into small strips about the size of matchsticks. Peel the garlic and chop finely or crush. Melt the butter in a large saucepan and fry the onion until it is soft. Add the carrots, beetroot, celeriac and garlic and fry gently for a few minutes. Sprinkle the sugar over the vegetables and add the wine vinegar. Pour in a little of the stock and bring to the boil, then reduce the heat to a simmer.

Remove any coarse outer leaves from the cabbage, cut it in half, remove the core, rinse, drain and shred finely. Scald the tomatoes in boiling water for 10 seconds, then peel, core and discard the seeds. Chop the flesh coarsely and place in the saucepan with the cabbage. Season lightly with salt, add the rest of the stock and simmer gently for 30 minutes.

Remove any fat from the beef. Cut the ham, sausages and beef into strips about 5 mm/¼ in wide. Place in the soup, season and continue to simmer for a further 30 minutes. Rinse the dill and shake dry. Adjust the seasoning, and pour into a large heated soup tureen. Pour the soured cream into the centre and serve, garnished with the dill.

1 **Skimming the stock.** Remove the grey scum which keeps forming on the surface of the stock, using a skimming spoon, so that the stock becomes as clear as possible.

2 **Preparing the cabbage.** Remove any coarse outer leaves, cut the cabbage in half and cut out the stalk with a sharp knife. Rinse and drain the cabbage, then shred finely.

3 **Adding the meat.** Place the strips of beef, ham and sausage in the stock with the vegetables. Season lightly with salt, but add a generous amount of black pepper.

Our tip

Beetroot is available from October to May. Buy it uncooked with the leaves or stalk still attached. Never buy it if all the stalks have been removed, otherwise it will bleed and lose most of its flavour. It is possible to freeze Borsch; in fact, it freezes admirably. Prepare it as described in the recipe but use slightly less seasoning and reduce the cooking time. When it has cooled, pack it into containers and freeze. Before using, place the Borsch in a saucepan with a little water and heat gently until thawed. Bring to the boil, season to taste and serve with the soured cream and dill.

Avocado Salad

Ripe avocados and smoked beef or ham give this salad a slightly nutty aroma that harmonises well with crisp lettuce and palm hearts.

---

1 (425-g/15-oz) can palm hearts
¼ Iceberg or Webb's Wonder
lettuce (about 225 g/8 oz)
100 g/4 oz button mushrooms
juice 1½ lemons
2 ripe avocados
(each weighing about 225 g/8 oz)
150 ml/¼ pint natural yoghurt
salt
freshly ground white pepper
pinch sugar
pinch cayenne pepper
few drops Worcestershire sauce
1–2 tablespoons gin
1 teaspoon nut oil
50 g/2 oz smoked beef or ham
(prosciutto), sliced very thinly
¼ punnet mustard and cress

Preparation time: 45 minutes

Drain the palm hearts and cut them diagonally into slices 1 cm/½ in wide. Rinse the lettuce thoroughly in cold water and shake dry in a salad basket or tea towel. Tear the leaves into small pieces. Clean the mushrooms and cut off the base of the stalks. Slice the mushrooms very thinly and sprinkle with lemon juice to prevent them going brown.

Cut the avocados in half by slicing them lengthways round the stone and twisting the two halves apart. Brush the cut surfaces at once with lemon juice to prevent discoloration. Score the avocado skins lengthways with a sharp knife and pull off the skin in strips. Brush the exposed surfaces with lemon juice. Put half an avocado aside for the dressing and cut the rest crossways into slices 5 mm/¼ in thick. Sprinkle with lemon juice again.

Mash the reserved avocado half and pass through a plastic sieve if necessary to make the purée smooth (the sieve used should on no account be made of metal which would cause the avocado to discolour). Mix the avocado purée with the yoghurt and the rest of the lemon juice, and season to taste with salt, pepper, sugar, cayenne pepper and Worcestershire sauce. Beat the gin and nut oil into the dressing drop by drop and season again if necessary; the dressing should be piquant in flavour.

Arrange the lettuce, avocado slices, palm hearts and mushrooms on a large salad plate or as individual portions on smaller plates. Loosely roll the beef or ham slices and arrange them round the edges of the salad. Place the dressing on top of the salad; do not mix it with the ingredients. Rinse the cress under cold running water, shake dry and cut off the tiny leaves with a pair of scissors. Sprinkle over the salad as a garnish and serve immediately.

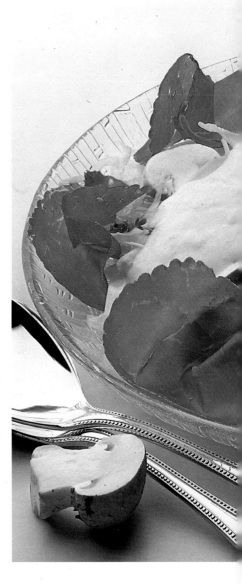

1 **Halve the avocados** by cutting them lengthways round the stone and twisting the two halves apart. Do this gently to avoid bruising the avocado flesh.

2 **Peeling the avocados.** Score the skins lengthways with a sharp knife and strip off the skin. Brush the surface of the fruit with lemon juice.

3 **Cleaning the mushrooms.** Trim the stalks and wipe the tops with a damp cloth. Slice very thinly and sprinkle with lemon juice to prevent them going brown.

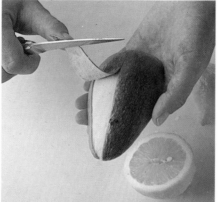

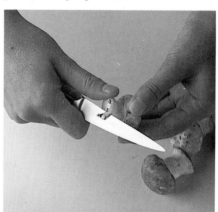

4 **Preparing the dressing.** Mix the avocado purée, yoghurt, the rest of the lemon juice and the seasonings together. Beat in the gin and nut oil very gradually and season again to make sure that the dressing is piquant enough.

Our tip

Only use ripe avocados for this salad as only ripe fruit has that delicate nutty flavour that goes so well with the other ingredients. Gently squeeze the fruit in the palm of your hand to test for ripeness. It will give a little if it is ripe. If only hard avocados are available, buy them a few days beforehand, wrap them in newspaper and leave them to ripen in a warm place.

Salade Nouvelle with Goose Liver

If you wish to eat as well at home as you would in an exclusive restaurant, try this nouvelle cuisine recipe for a salad with fried goose liver slices. Serve it simply with fresh French bread and a glass of white port or medium dry sherry.

100 g/4 oz French or Kenya green beans
salt
handful leaves curly endive
4 leaves red radicchio
12 leaves young spinach
½ large ripe tomato
8 button mushrooms
juice ½ lemon
small pinch sugar
freshly ground white pepper
1–2 teaspoons sherry vinegar
1 teaspoon blackcurrant or raspberry vinegar
2 tablespoons olive oil
1 teaspoon hazelnut or walnut oil
1½ tablespoons white port or medium dry sherry
½ canned truffle (optional)
225 g/8 oz fresh artificially fattened goose liver or canned pâté de fois gras

Preparation time: 30 minutes

Trim the beans and break them into pieces about 4 cm/1½ in in length. Cook them in boiling salted water for 3–4 minutes, then drain in a sieve. They should be just tender but still crisp. Pour ice-cold water over them to refresh them, then put aside to drain and cool.

Rinse the endive, radicchio and spinach leaves very thoroughly under cold running water. Shake them dry in a salad basket or clean tea towel. Scald the tomato in boiling water for 10 seconds, then peel and remove any core or hard green stem. Take tomato half in palm of your hand and squeeze gently until seeds fall out, then discard them. Slice the tomato into thin strips. Clean the mushrooms. Slice them very finely and sprinkle with lemon juice.

To make the dressing, mix together a good pinch of salt, the sugar and a little pepper with the sherry and blackcurrant or raspberry vinegars. Beat in the olive and nut oil gradually, then add the port or sherry and a few drops of liquid from the truffle can, if available.

Drain the truffle of any excess liquid and cut it first into thin slices and then into very fine strips. Scrape or peel the skin from the fresh liver, then cut it into slices about 1 cm/½ in thick. Heat a frying pan and without using any fat, fry the liver slices on both sides, allowing about 30 seconds for each side. Remove from the pan immediately and place on kitchen paper to drain off any excess fat. If you are using pâté, this should be sliced but not fried.

Toss each salad ingredient separately in the dressing and arrange with the slices of liver and the truffle strips on four dinner plates. As in the illustration, the dish should not only be a delicacy for the palate but a pleasure for the eye as well.

1 **Drying the salad.** Place the rinsed spinach, radicchio and endive leaves in a clean tea towel or salad basket and shake them to remove excess liquid.

2 **Preparing the mushrooms.** Clean the mushrooms and slice very thinly. Sprinkle them with the juice of half a lemon to prevent them turning brown.

3 **Preparing the truffle.** Drain the truffle of any excess liquid in the can and cut it into very thin slices with a sharp knife; then cut the slices into very thin strips.

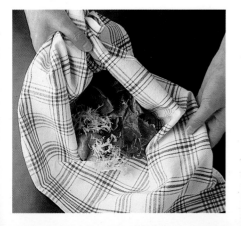 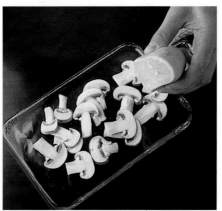 

4 **Removing the skin from the liver.** Take a sharp knife and scrape or peel off the skin. Cut the liver into slices about 1 cm/½ in thick. (Cut pâté into the same size slices.)

Our tip

Artificially fattened goose livers are an expensive delicacy. Fortunately, good quality goose livers from Israel are now available. They have a slightly stronger flavour than their French counterparts, but that is not a disadvantage. If fresh goose livers are not available, however, slices of canned pâté de foie gras may be used instead. The slices of pâté should not be fried.

Stuffed Peppers

Here are four different recipes for stuffed peppers which are all prepared in basically the same way; the preparation of the different fillings is a theme with variations, but the cooking of the stuffed peppers remains the same. The pepper at the back of the pan is stuffed with rice and turkey, on the right with lamb and rice, centre front with a mixture of minced pork and beef and on the left with a mushroom and cheese filling.

---

4 peppers of about the same size
2 tablespoons oil · 25 g/1 oz butter
6 tablespoons chicken stock
4 tablespoons dry white wine
2 tablespoons double or
soured cream

For the rice and turkey stuffing:
100 g/4 oz patna rice
3 tablespoons olive oil · 1 onion
2 slices turkey breast,
each weighing about
150 g/5 oz
2 large ripe tomatoes
25 g/1 oz sultanas or raisins
25 g/1 oz shelled pistachio nuts
salt · freshly ground white pepper
cayenne pepper · little lemon juice
$\frac{1}{2}$ bunch fresh parsley
1 sprig fresh thyme
$\frac{1}{2}$ teaspoon saffron powder
6 tablespoons hot chicken stock

Preparation time: 1$\frac{1}{2}$ hours

Prepare the peppers by cutting off the tops about 1 cm/$\frac{1}{2}$ in below the stalk. Twist out the cores and cut out the inner partitions. Rinse under cold water, making sure that all the seeds have been removed, and pat dry.

To make the stuffing, place the rice in a sieve, rinse under cold running water and pat dry in a tea towel. Heat the oil in a saucepan and fry the rice gently for 5 minutes or until it is translucent. Peel and finely chop the onion. Cut the turkey meat into tiny strips. Add both to the rice. Scald the tomatoes in boiling water for 10 seconds, then peel and remove the core and any piece of hard stem. Cut the tomatoes in half so that all seed chambers are visible and squeeze gently until the seeds fall out. Discard these and chop the flesh. Rinse the sultanas in hot water and pat dry. Place the tomatoes, sultanas and pistachio nuts in the pan and season to

taste with salt, pepper, cayenne pepper and lemon juice. Wash the herbs, shake dry and chop very finely. Stir into the other ingredients in the pan. Dissolve the saffron in the hot stock, then pour into the pan. Bring the stock quickly to the boil, stirring constantly, then reduce the heat and simmer gently until the rice has absorbed all the liquid and is almost tender.

Using a teaspoon, fill the peppers with the rice mixture, pressing it down lightly with the back of the spoon. Heat the oil and butter in a flameproof casserole and place the peppers in the fat. Put the tops on the peppers and pour the stock and wine into the casserole. Cover and simmer gently for 40 minutes or until tender. Remove the peppers and keep warm. Stir the cream into the liquid in the casserole and boil to reduce a little. Pour this sauce into a heated serving dish, place the peppers in the sauce and serve.

Lamb and Rice Stuffing. Cook 100 g/4 oz patna rice in boiling salted water for 10 minutes, then drain in a sieve and rinse it under cold running water. Drain and put aside to cool. Peel 2 onions and 2 cloves of garlic and chop finely. Fry both gently in 1 tablespoon of olive oil until they are soft and golden. Set aside to cool.

Mix together 450 g/1 lb minced lamb, the onion, garlic and rice. Season generously with salt, black pepper and $\frac{1}{4}$ teaspoon of ground cinnamon. Rinse 3 sprigs of fresh mint, shake dry and chop finely. Stir into the mixture. Stuff and cook the peppers as described in the basic recipe.

Minced Meat Stuffing. Soften a stale bread roll in water, then squeeze out the excess water and crumble the roll into small pieces. Peel 1 onion and 1–2 cloves of garlic and chop both finely. Mix the bread, onion and garlic with 450 g/1 lb minced meat (preferably a mixture of beef and pork). Rinse, dry and chop a bunch of parsley. Stir it into the mixture with $\frac{1}{2}$–1 tablespoon green peppercorns. Season to taste with salt and black pepper and a dash each of Worcestershire and Tabasco sauces. Stuff and cook the peppers as described in the basic recipe.

Mushroom and Cheese Stuffing. Peel and chop 1 onion and 1 clove of garlic. Clean and chop 350 g/12 oz mushrooms. Fry the onion, garlic and mushrooms in 2 tablespoons oil until soft and transparent. Add

75 g/3 oz patna rice and fry gently until all the oil has been absorbed. Scald 2 tomatoes in boiling water for 10 seconds, then peel and chop. Rinse dry and chop a few sprigs of parsley. Add the tomatoes and parsley to the rice mixture with 6 tablespoons stock and 2 tablespoons lemon juice. Season to taste with salt and pepper and cook for 10 minutes or until the rice is almost cooked.

Meanwhile, rinse, dry and chop 3 sprigs of fresh basil. Grate 40 g/1$\frac{1}{2}$ oz Parmesan cheese. Add the basil and cheese to the rice mixture and combine thoroughly. Stuff and cook the peppers as described in the basic recipe.

1 **Preparing the peppers.** Cut off the tops of the peppers about 1 cm/½ in below the stalk. Twist out the cores and cut out the inner partitions.

2 **Pouring in the stock.** Dissolve the saffron in the hot stock and pour over the rice, stirring the mixture all the time. Bring rapidly to the boil, then simmer gently.

3 **Filling the peppers.** Use a teaspoon to stuff the peppers and press the mixture down lightly with the back of the spoon. Heat the oil and butter in a flameproof casserole.

4 **Cooking the peppers.** Place the peppers in the hot fat and press the tops in place. Pour the stock and dry white wine into the casserole. Cover and simmer until tender.

Gratin Dauphinois

This famous French potato dish goes well with lamb and other grilled meats or can be eaten as a light meal accompanied by a mixed salad.

---

800 g/1¾ lb floury potatoes
1–2 cloves garlic
50 g/2 oz butter
salt
freshly ground black pepper
grated nutmeg
75 g/3 oz Gruyère or
Emmental cheese
750 ml/1¼ pints double cream

Preparation time: 1¼ hours

Heat the oven to moderately hot (200°C, 400°F, gas 6). Peel the potatoes and cut into slices about 3 mm/⅛ in thick. Lay the slices on kitchen paper and pat dry. Peel the garlic and cut in half. Rub a shallow baking dish with the cut sides of the garlic to give the dish a pleasant aroma, then discard the garlic. Butter the dish generously, using half the butter. Put the potatoes in layers in the dish so that they overlap one another and season each layer with salt, pepper and nutmeg. The potatoes should not be higher than 2.5–4 cm/1–1½ in in the dish and there should be a gap of at least 1 cm/½ in at the top so that the cream cannot boil over.

Grate the cheese and sprinkle over the potatoes evenly. Pour over the cream, making sure that all the gaps are filled. The potatoes should be covered with cream – it may be necessary to increase the amount of cream if the dish is large. Dot the remaining butter over the potatoes. Place in the middle of the heated oven. Depending on the type of potato used, the dish will take 45–60 minutes to cook. Test with a fork after 45 minutes to see if the potatoes are tender. If the potatoes are ready and the surface is golden and crisp, the gratin can be served. If the surface gets too brown before the potatoes are cooked through, cover with foil or greaseproof paper.

1 **Rubbing the dish with garlic.** Rub a shallow baking dish with the cut sides of the garlic. This will give the cooked potatoes a pleasant aroma without a strong garlic flavour.

2 **Putting the potatoes in the dish.** Put the potato slices in the dish so that they overlap one another. Season each layer with salt, pepper and grated nutmeg.

3 **Pouring in the cream.** Pour the cream over the potatoes and grated cheese so that any spaces between the potatoes are filled. The potatoes should be completely covered with cream.

Our tip

Instead of cream, a mixture of milk and double cream, or milk and single cream with beaten eggs, can be used. The quantity of cheese can also be increased or decreased according to taste. The potatoes used should be of a floury variety and preferably of the same size so that the slices cook evenly.

Beetroot and Broccoli Creams

These delicious little moulded vegetable creams served with a cool cream sauce make an admirable hors d'oeuvre or appetiser. They can also be served with meat instead of the usual vegetables but then, of course, without the cream sauce.

---

450 g/1 lb fresh green sprouting
broccoli
salt
350 g/12 oz beetroot (weighed
without stalks and leaves)
50 g/2 oz butter
450 ml/¾ pint double cream
butter for greasing dishes
2 eggs
2 egg whites
freshly ground white pepper
sugar
lemon juice

For the cream sauce:
2 tablespoons soured cream
4 tablespoons double cream
1 tablespoon sherry vinegar
salt
freshly ground white pepper
1 shallot
small bunch chives

Preparation time: 1½ hours

Discard any coarse stalks from the broccoli and divide the tiny florets – about 350 g/12 oz should remain. Bring a large saucepan of salted water to the boil, add the broccoli and blanch for 3 minutes. Drain and plunge into ice-cold water. Leave the broccoli in a sieve to drain and cool. Peel the beetroot and cut into thin slices.

Heat the oven to moderate (160°C, 325°F, gas 3). Heat half of the butter in one saucepan and the remaining butter in another. Place the broccoli in one pan and the beetroot in the other and fry gently, stirring frequently, until the vegetables become a little glassy in appearance. Add half of the cream to each pan and bring to the boil. Reduce the heat and cook gently for a further 10 minutes or until the vegetables are soft. The liquid should also have reduced a little.

Meanwhile, butter eight individual ovenproof moulds or ramekins and place in the refrigerator.

The vegetables must now be reduced to a purée. Place the broccoli mixture in the goblet of a blender or food processor and add an egg and an egg white. Season to taste with salt, pepper, a pinch of sugar and a little lemon juice. Turn the machine to the highest speed and process until the mixture is light and frothy in consistency. Alternatively, sieve the broccoli mixture to a purée, then whisk in the egg, egg white and seasonings.

Take half the moulds out of the refrigerator and rub with butter again. Fill with the broccoli mixture. Purée the beetroot mixture with the remaining egg, egg white and seasonings, and fill the remaining moulds in the same way.

Place a thick layer of greaseproof paper or newspaper on the bottom of a large baking tin and stand the moulds on the paper. Pour in enough hot water to come halfway up the sides of the moulds. Bake in the heated oven for 55–60 minutes.

Meanwhile, prepare the cream sauce. Stir together the soured cream, double cream and sherry vinegar and season to taste with salt and pepper. Peel the shallot and chop it finely. Rinse the chives, shake dry and cut into very short lengths with scissors. Stir the shallot and chives into the sauce and place in the refrigerator to chill until it is served.

When the creams are ready, remove them from the tin of water. Run a sharp knife round the edges so that they do not stick and turn them out on to a heated serving plate or on to individual plates. Mop up any excess melted butter with kitchen paper. Pour a little of the sauce over each cream and serve immediately.

1 Pouring in the cream. As soon as the vegetables become slightly glassy, pour half the cream into each pan and bring to the boil. Cook gently for 10 minutes.

2 Blending the vegetables. Place the broccoli, the liquid in which it was cooked, an egg and an egg white in the blender or food processor. Season and purée.

3 Placing the moulds in the baking tin. Put a thick layer of greaseproof paper or newspaper on the bottom of the baking tin and stand the moulds on it.

4 Removing the creams. Run a sharp knife round the edges of the creams to loosen them. Turn on to a serving plate or individual plates. Pour a little sauce over each one and serve immediately.

Our tip

The moulds or ramekins must be buttered generously so that the delicate vegetable creams do not stick to the sides when being turned out on to the plates. Rub generously with softened butter and chill in the refrigerator so that the butter hardens before buttering again before use. This will ensure a smooth surface to the turned-out creams.

Stuffed Artichokes

Crisp on the outside and juicy on the inside – that is how these stuffed artichokes should be when you serve them, with a glass of chilled dry white or rosé wine. The artichoke leaves, with filling, should be pulled off and eaten with the fingers and the base with a knife and fork.

4 large globe artichokes
juice 1–2 lemons
1 thick slice white bread
3–4 tablespoons milk
1 shallot
1 clove garlic
small bunch fresh parsley
3 anchovy fillets
25 g/1 oz lean cooked ham
25 g/1 oz Gruyère or
Emmental cheese
salt
freshly ground white pepper
6 tablespoons olive oil
450 ml/¾ pint dry white wine

Preparation time: 1½ hours

Heat the oven to moderate (180°C, 350°F, gas 4). Remove the stalks from the artichokes by bending the stalks back and forth until they break off, or cut off using a sharp knife. Remove the hard threads from the base at the same time. Neaten the base and edges with a sharp knife and brush the cut surfaces with lemon juice to prevent discoloration. Cut off the tops of the artichokes about one-third of the distance from the tip. Trim off any remaining pointed leaves with kitchen scissors. Brush the cut edges with lemon juice. Place the artichokes upside-down on the working surface and press a few times until the leaves start to bend. Pull apart the centre leaves and scoop out the hairy 'choke' using a spoon. Rub all round the cut surfaces of the artichokes with lemon juice once more and put aside.

Now make the stuffing. Remove the crust from the slice of bread. Pour milk over the bread and leave to soak for 5 minutes. Peel the shallot and garlic and chop finely. Rinse the parsley, shake it dry and chop. If the anchovy fillets are very salty, they should be soaked in cold water for a while or rinsed under cold running water. Pat dry, then crush or chop them. Cut the ham into tiny cubes (about 3 mm/⅛ in). Grate the cheese. Squeeze the bread to remove excess milk and place in a bowl with the shallot, garlic, parsley, anchovies, ham and cheese. Mix to a smooth creamy paste. Season to taste with salt and pepper.

Stuff the artichokes, working from the outer leaves towards the centre. The leaves should be pliable enough to be pulled away from one another.

Heat 2 tablespoons of the oil in a shallow flameproof dish. Place the artichokes in the dish and sprinkle with the remaining oil. Pour the wine into the dish, cover and place in the middle of the heated oven. Bake for 40–60 minutes, basting frequently with the wine in the dish. The artichokes are ready when the bases are soft (test with a skewer). Then increase the oven temperature to hot (220°C, 425°F, gas 7) and cook for a further 5 minutes or until the artichokes become crisp and brown. Serve hot.

Our tip

If possible, use tender young artichokes for this dish; older ones can take up to 2 hours to cook and easily become dry in the process. Young artichokes can be recognised by their stalks – the smaller the artichoke is in comparison with the stalk, the younger it is. If only older artichokes are available, it is advisable to cook them for a few minutes in simmering water, with a little lemon juice added, before proceeding as described in the recipe.

1 **Removing the stalk.** Bend the stalk back and forth until it breaks and pull the threads out of the base at the same time. Neaten the base and edges with a sharp knife.

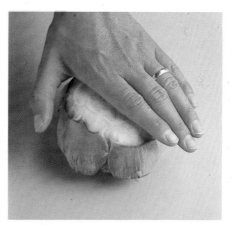

2 **Opening the leaves.** Place the artichokes upside down on the work surface and press them until the leaves begin to bend. Brush all over with lemon juice.

3 **Filling the artichokes.** Starting with the outer leaves, bend the leaves apart and stuff the spaces in between. Heat the olive oil in a shallow flameproof dish.

Home-made Spaghetti in Gorgonzola Cream

The fresh flavour of home-made pasta is incomparably better than anything a factory can produce and those who have made pasta once will find it is well worth making again.

---

400 g/14 oz plain flour
4 eggs
2 tablespoons olive oil
salt
225 g/8 oz Gorgonzola cheese
15 g/½ oz butter
250 ml/8 fl oz single cream
freshly ground black pepper
2 sprigs fresh basil

Resting time for the dough:
about 1 hour
Preparation time: 1 hour

Sift the flour on to the work surface and make a hollow in the middle. Beat the eggs and the oil together, season with a generous pinch of salt and pour into the depression in the flour. Work the ingredients together. As soon as it is a coherent mass, the pasta machine can be used for the hard task of kneading the dough.

Set the machine at the widest roller setting and roll the dough through the machine. Fold three times, then turn at a right angle and put the dough through the machine again. Dust with flour from time to time and repeat the process again and again until the dough is smooth and silky looking (eight to ten times is usually sufficient). Cover the dough and leave to rest for 30 minutes (this increases the elasticity of the dough).

Cut the dough into four portions. Knead each portion again, as in the first stage, meanwhile keeping the other portions covered so that they do not dry out.

Put all the dough together again and put it through the machine at the widest roller setting. Decrease the setting gradually, rolling the dough again and again until it is very thin. It is easier when two people do this job – one putting the dough through the machine and the other turning the handle, and both catching and holding the dough as it emerges at the other end.

When the dough is thin enough, change the setting on the machine to use the narrow groove cutting roller. Put the dough through the machine in portions and let the spaghetti noodles run over the back of the hand as they emerge. Drape them over an indoor washing line or a clean broomstick laid between two kitchen chairs and let them dry for 20 minutes.

To make the sauce, chop the cheese into small pieces and place in a heavy saucepan with the butter. Melt over a gentle heat, stirring all the time to prevent the cheese sticking or burning. As soon as the cheese has melted, stir in the cream. Grind a little pepper over the sauce. Keep it warm in a bain marie, or by putting the saucepan in a larger pan containing hot water, while boiling the noodles.

Bring 4.5 litres/1 gallon of salted water to the boil in a large saucepan. Place the noodles in the boiling water and cook for 1 minute. Drain in a large sieve or colander, shaking well to remove excess water. Put the drained noodles into the cream sauce and toss and turn them gently with two forks so that all strands are coated with the sauce. Divide between four heated plates and grind a little pepper over each portion. Rinse the basil and shake dry. Garnish each portion of spaghetti with a few basil leaves and serve hot.

1 **Kneading the dough.** Roll the dough through the machine at the widest roller setting. Fold it into three, turn it 90° and put it through the machine again.

2 **Rolling the dough.** Gradually reduce the roller setting so that the dough becomes thinner and thinner. The dough should not be folded again.

3 **Preparing the sauce.** Cut the cheese into small pieces and place in the pan with the butter. Melt over a gentle heat, stirring all the time, then add the cream.

4 **Put the spaghetti in the sauce.** Pull apart a little with two forks and turn so that all the strands are coated with sauce. Spoon on to plates, sprinkle with pepper and garnish with basil.

Our tip

If you use a pasta machine, you will need someone to help with the rolling and cutting of the long noodles. If you wish to try the recipe and do not have a pasta machine, knead the dough by hand at the first stage until it is smooth and elastic. Rest the dough and then roll out small portions on a floured surface until they are very thin. Cut into thin strips, or roll up and cut into thin strips before unrolling the separate strands.

Stuffed Onions

These onions with their hearty kale or spinach stuffing go particularly well with pork dishes and roast goose or duck.

450 g/1 lb winter kale or spinach
salt
4 large onions (each weighing about 400 g/14 oz)
freshly ground black pepper
pinch sugar
75 g/3 oz goose fat or lard
3–4 tablespoons hot meat stock
25 g/1 oz fresh breadcrumbs

Preparation time: 1½ hours

Remove the kale or spinach leaves from the stalks and rinse them thoroughly in cold water. Blanch in boiling salted water for 5 minutes. Tip the kale or spinach into a colander and rinse under cold running water. Drain well, then chop as finely as possible.

Heat the oven to moderately hot (200°C, 400°F, gas 6). Meanwhile, fill a second saucepan with salted water and bring to the boil. Peel the onions and place in the boiling water. Cook for about 5–10 minutes or until they are just tender – the cooking time depends on the size of the onions. Drain well and allow to cool.

Cut a 'lid' from the top of each onion and press out the centres with the fingertips so that only two or three outside layers remain. Chop the 'lids' and centres as finely as possible. Mix the chopped onion into the spinach or kale. Season to taste with salt, pepper and sugar. Melt about 25 g/1 oz of the goose fat or lard in a saucepan and add the kale or spinach mixture with the stock, then cover and cook for 5 minutes.

Grease an ovenproof dish with a little of the remaining goose fat or lard. Stuff the onions with the kale or spinach mixture, heaping it up on top. Sprinkle with the breadcrumbs and dot with the rest of the goose fat or lard. Place the onions in the dish and then in the heated oven. Bake for 15 minutes, then reduce the temperature to cool (150°C, 300°F, gas 2). Bake for a further 10–15 minutes.

Serve the onions as soon as they are ready so that none of the delicious aroma – due to the goose fat – is lost.

Our tip

The amount of filling needed will depend on the size of the onions. If the onions are small, provide two per person. If any filling is left over, spread it over the bottom of the dish and make little depressions to stand each onion in. Sprinkle the leftover stuffing with breadcrumbs and dot with goose fat or lard so that it does not become dry.

1 Removing the centres of the onions. Press out the centre of each onion so that only two or three outside layers remain. Chop the centres very finely and mix with the kale or spinach.

2 Cooking the kale or spinach. Heat the goose fat or lard in a saucepan. Add the kale or spinach mixture and stock, then cover and cook for 5 minutes.

3 Stuffing the onions. Place the kale or spinach mixture in the hollowed-out onions, mounding it up on top. Sprinkle with breadcrumbs and dot with goose fat or lard.

Aubergines with Tsatsiki

Aubergines with tsatsiki is a Greek speciality which has rapidly gained in popularity in Europe in recent years. It is a light summer dish that can be served as a starter or as a light snack.

---

800 g/1¾ lb aubergines of about
the same size
salt
300 ml/½ pint natural yoghurt
juice ½ lemon
2–3 cloves garlic
½ bunch fresh dill
½ cucumber
freshly ground white pepper
· flour
6–8 tablespoons olive oil

Preparation time: 45 minutes

Rinse and dry the aubergines and trim off the ends. Cut the aubergines on a slant into slices 1 cm/½ in thick. Lay the slices next to one another on a plate and sprinkle both sides with salt. Leave for about 20 minutes to allow excess moisture and bitter juices to be drawn out.

During this time the tsatsiki can be prepared. Mix the yoghurt with the lemon juice. Peel the garlic and chop as finely as possible or crush over the yoghurt with a garlic press. Rinse the dill, shake dry and chop finely. Stir into the yoghurt with the garlic. Wipe the cucumber and grate over the mixture. Season generously with salt and pepper, then beat vigorously with a balloon whisk until the tsatsiki is light and frothy. The process of beating will distribute and enhance the flavours of the ingredients. Cover the dish and put in the refrigerator to chill.

Rinse the aubergine slices and pat dry with kitchen paper. Dust each slice with flour. This is best done by pressing both sides of each slice into the flour and shaking off the excess flour afterwards. Heat a few tablespoons of oil in a frying pan and fry the aubergines, a few slices at a time, over a high heat until they are golden brown on both sides. Add more oil to the pan if necessary. Turn the slices only once to prevent them breaking. Remove from the pan and drain on kitchen paper. Pat the upper surfaces with kitchen paper as well so that all the oil is removed; aubergines tend to absorb a good deal of oil during frying.

Serve the aubergines hot or cold with the tsatsiki poured over them. Fresh French bread and well-drained black olives make excellent accompaniments.

1 **Salt the aubergines.** Lay the slices next to one another and sprinkle salt on both sides. Leave them to allow the bitter juices and excess moisture to be drawn out.

2 **Preparing the tsatsiki.** Grate the cucumber over the yoghurt. Season to taste with salt and pepper. Beat well with a balloon whisk to distribute the flavours evenly, and chill.

3 **Frying the aubergines.** Heat the oil in a frying pan and fry the aubergine, a few slices at a time, until both sides are golden brown. Drain well on kitchen paper.

Our tip

Courgettes can be prepared in the same way and served with tsatsiki. The process of sprinkling with salt can be omitted unless the courgettes are very watery.

Lasagne Verdi al Forno

The hearts of pasta lovers everywhere beat faster at the thought of Lasagne al Forno. This versatile dish can be served as a main course with salad or as a starter. As the latter this quantity will serve 10 people.

Serves 6

50 g/2 oz streaky bacon
1 onion
1 clove garlic
1 stick celery
1 carrot
2 large ripe tomatoes
2 tablespoons olive oil
150 g/5 oz mixed minced
pork and beef
6 tablespoons hot stock
little red wine
1 tablespoon tomato purée
salt
freshly ground black pepper
pinch sugar
2 sprigs fresh oregano
2 sprigs fresh parsley
65 g/2½ oz butter
65 g/2½ oz plain flour
750 ml/1¼ pints hot milk
grated nutmeg
225 g/8 oz mozzarella cheese
75 g/3 oz Parmesan cheese
butter for greasing dish
5 tablespoons cream
about 225 g/8 oz green lasagne
(see tip)

Preparation time: 2 hours

The meat sauce should be prepared first. Trim the rind from the bacon and chop into small pieces. Peel the onion and garlic. Trim the celery and peel or scrape the carrot. Chop all the vegetables into very small dice. Scald the tomatoes in boiling water for 10 seconds, then peel and remove the core and any pieces of hard stem. Cut the tomatoes in half so that all seed chambers are visible and, taking half a tomato at a time in the palm of your hand, squeeze gently until the seeds fall out. Discard, and chop the tomatoes very finely.

Put the bacon in a large saucepan and fry until the fat runs out. Add the olive oil and then the onion, garlic, celery and carrot. Fry, stirring all the time, until the vegetables are softened and any moisture has evaporated. Add the minced meat and fry until it becomes browned and crumbly in appearance. Stir in the tomatoes, stock, red wine and tomato purée. Season to taste with salt, pepper and sugar and bring to the boil quickly.

Rinse the oregano and parsley, shake dry and chop finely. Stir the herbs into the sauce, then reduce the heat and simmer gently for 20 minutes, stirring occasionally.

While the meat sauce is cooking, prepare the béchamel sauce. Melt the butter in a saucepan and stir in the flour. Cook for 1 minute, then gradually add the hot milk, stirring all the time. Bring to the boil, stirring, and simmer for 10 minutes. Season with a little grated nutmeg and salt and pepper to taste.

Chop the mozzarella cheese into small pieces. Grate the Parmesan cheese. Grease a rectangular baking dish with butter. Heat the oven to moderately hot (200°C, 400°F, gas 6). When the meat sauce is ready, stir in the cream.

To assemble the lasagne, start with a thin layer of béchamel sauce in the baking dish and cover with sheets of pasta. Then add a thin layer of meat sauce which should be spread out evenly. Pour another layer of béchamel sauce over the meat sauce, and sprinkle a little Parmesan cheese and a few pieces of mozzarella cheese over it. Place a few more sheets of pasta on top of the cheese, making sure that they do not overlap. Continue the

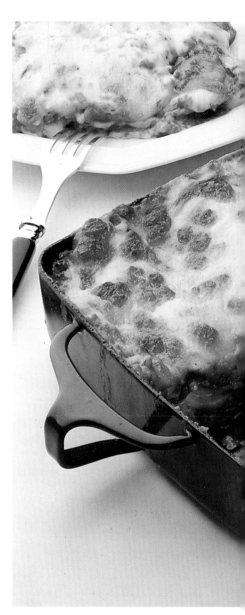

layers, finishing with béchamel sauce and cheese. Place in the heated oven and bake for 25–30 minutes. Serve immediately.

Our tip

Read the instructions for the pasta carefully before preparing the dish – some pasta needs to be precooked. If this is the case, rinse the sheets of pasta under cold running water after cooking and spread them out on a clean tea towel to drain thoroughly. Start with a layer of pasta when assembling the ingredients in the dish. If it is not necessary to precook the pasta, the first layer should always be of béchamel sauce.

1 **Seasoning the béchamel sauce.** Season the sauce with a little freshly grated nutmeg and salt, but a generous amount of pepper, and whisk briefly to combine.

2 **Spreading the meat sauce.** Spread out a thin layer of meat sauce evenly on top of the pasta using a flat spoon or spatula. Be sure all the pasta is covered.

3 **Adding the béchamel sauce.** Pour a little sauce over the meat sauce and sprinkle with a little Parmesan cheese and a few pieces of mozzarella cheese.

4 **Arranging the lasagne.** Lay the sheets of lasagne next to one another on top of the layer of cheese. The final layer should be of béchamel sauce and cheese.

Baked Chicory with Ham

Baked chicory wrapped in ham is a dish for all occasions. It can be served as a starter during a full-scale dinner or as part of a light meal.

---

4 heads chicory
40 g/1½ oz butter
6 tablespoons hot chicken stock
juice ½ lemon
salt
freshly ground white pepper
grated nutmeg
150 ml/¼ pint double cream
4 slices cooked ham
100 g/4 oz Gruyère or
Emmental cheese

Preparation time: 45 minutes

Remove any of the outer leaves from the chicory which are brown or wilted. Rinse and pat dry. Take each head and cut a small wedge-shaped piece from the base, without damaging the outer leaves. This part of the vegetable contains the bitter substances which sometimes give it an overwhelming flavour.

Heat the oven to hot (220°C, 425°F, gas 7). Grease an oval ovenproof dish with 15 g/½ oz of the butter. Place the rest of the butter in a frying pan and add the chicory. Cook gently over a moderate heat, turning occasionally. As soon as the outer leaves become a little transparent – they should not change colour – add the hot chicken stock and lemon juice. Season to taste with salt, pepper and nutmeg. Bring to the boil, then stir in the cream, being careful not to damage the chicory. Cover the pan and cook gently for a further 5–6 minutes.

Place a slice of ham on a round skimming spoon. Remove a head of chicory from the pan with a fork. Allow the excess sauce to drip off, then place the chicory on the ham and roll it up. Hold the skimming spoon over the pan during this process so that any sauce from the chicory drips back into the pan. Place each chicory and ham roll in the ovenproof dish.

Turn up the heat under the frying pan and boil the sauce until it has reduced to about half the quantity. Season again with salt, pepper and nutmeg. Grate the cheese and stir half into the sauce until melted and smooth. Pour the sauce over the chicory and ham rolls, shaking the dish to distribute the sauce evenly. Sprinkle the remaining cheese over the top so that the surface is well covered. Place the dish on the middle shelf of the heated oven and bake for 15 minutes. Serve immediately or the cheese will lose a lot of its flavour.

New potatoes with chopped parsley or creamed potato with herbs go well with this dish.

1 **Removing the bitter core.** Cut a small wedge-shaped piece out of the base of each head of chicory without damaging the outer leaves. This part of the vegetable is quite bitter.

2 **Wrapping the chicory.** Remove each head of chicory from the pan with a fork, allow excess sauce to drain off, then lay the chicory on the ham and roll up.

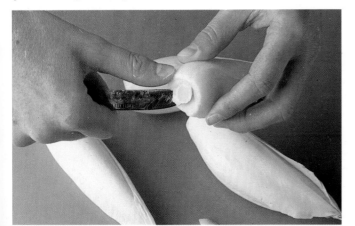

3 **Sprinkling over the cheese.** If the cheese is distributed evenly over the chicory and ham rolls, it will brown evenly and develop its full aroma. Bake until melted and golden.

Our tip

It is possible to make this dish with other vegetables, for example salsify or leeks. If the vegetables used are thin, wrap more than one piece in each slice of ham. The recipe is particularly good made with asparagus or canned palm hearts. Other kinds of ham can also be used; try prosciutto, or smoked ham, or ham cooked in wine or flavoured with herbs.

Cheese Soufflé

Not only experts succeed in producing a good soufflé – it is no problem for the beginner either. Make sure there are no draughts in the kitchen and serve it straight from the oven.

---

butter for greasing dish
100 g/4 oz Gruyère cheese
65 g/2½ oz butter
65 g/2½ oz plain flour
300 ml/½ pint milk
salt
freshly ground white pepper
grated nutmeg
4 eggs, separated

Preparation time: 1 hour

Butter a soufflé dish (about 20 cm/8 in in diameter). Grate the cheese, and sprinkle a little over the inside of the dish. Heat the oven to moderately hot (200°C, 400°F, gas 6). Melt the butter in a saucepan and stir in the flour. Cook, stirring, for 1–2 minutes or until the mixture has become creamy in colour and a little frothy. It should not become brown. Gradually stir in the hot milk and continue stirring until it is well blended. Bring to the boil and simmer, stirring, until the sauce becomes thick and creamy. Season to taste with salt, pepper and nutmeg. Remove from the heat and allow to cool slightly.

Add the egg yolks to the sauce, one at a time. It is important that each yolk is beaten into the sauce thoroughly before the next is added so that the mixture is perfectly smooth. When all the yolks have been beaten in, pour the mixture into a large bowl.

Put 1 teaspoon of the remaining cheese aside for later use and stir the rest into the mixture until melted and smooth. Beat the egg whites in a separate bowl until stiff peaks form. Tip the egg white on to the cheese mixture and fold in gently but quickly, using a metal spoon. Do not stir or the air beaten into the egg whites will be lost.

Spoon the mixture without delay into the soufflé dish; it should come about halfway up the sides of the dish, leaving enough room to rise. Sprinkle the reserved cheese over the top and place in the heated oven on the second shelf from the bottom. Bake for 25–30 minutes or until the surface is golden brown and the soufflé has risen above the rim of the dish. The soufflé should be a little creamy in the centre – on no account dry and hard. Remove from the oven and serve immediately.

1 **Making the roux.** Stirring all the time, blend the butter and flour together over a moderate heat until the paste is creamy in colour and a little frothy.

2 **Adding the milk.** Pour in the hot milk, a little at a time, and stir until the ingredients have blended well together. Continue to stir until the sauce becomes thick.

3 **Add the egg yolks singly.** It is important that each yolk is beaten separately into the mixture, so that it can be completely absorbed. Stir in the cheese.

4 **Folding in the egg whites.** Fold the egg whites into the mixture gently but quickly so that the mixture remains light and airy. Spoon the mixture into the dish.

Peanut Broccoli Flan

This delicious peanut pastry case with its broccoli, ham and cream filling, covered with crisp toasted cheese, makes an excellent light meal accompanied by a fresh white wine or lager.

Serves 8

---

100 g/4 oz roasted salted peanuts
225 g/8 oz plain flour · salt
good pinch cayenne pepper
7 eggs
2 tablespoons iced water
75 g/3 oz cold butter
1 kg/2 lb fresh broccoli
or 575 g/1¼ lb frozen broccoli
225 g/8 oz cooked ham
small bunch fresh parsley
450 ml/¾ pint single cream
75 g/3 oz Gruyère or Emmental cheese
freshly ground white pepper
grated nutmeg

Cooling time: 1 hour
Preparation time: 1½ hours

Place the peanuts in a polythene bag and crush them with a rolling pin or a heavy bottle until they are almost ground to a paste, or grind in a processor. Sift the flour on to a work surface and add the crushed peanuts, a pinch of salt and the cayenne pepper. Make a hollow in the centre. Break one of the eggs into the depression and add the iced water. Cut the butter into small pieces and place round the edges of the flour.

Knead the ingredients together to form a smooth dough, using your fingertips. Knead as quickly as possible so that the ingredients, particularly the butter, do not become warm. If they do, the resulting pastry may be heavy. Shape the dough into a ball, wrap in foil and place in the refrigerator to rest for 1 hour.

Meanwhile, prepare the filling. If fresh broccoli is to be used, remove any wilted leaves or hard stalks. Rinse and drain, then separate the tiny florets. Chop the tender stalks into short pieces. Cook the broccoli florets and stalks in boiling salted water for 8–10 minutes. Frozen broccoli can be placed unthawed in

boiling salted water and cooked for 4 minutes. Drain and rinse under cold running water. Drain again and put aside to cool.

Heat the oven to moderately hot (200°C, 400°F, gas 6). Remove any fat from the ham and cut it into strips. Rinse the parsley, shake it dry and chop finely. Beat the remaining eggs together and stir in the cream. Grate the cheese and stir half of it into the egg mixture. Season generously with salt and pepper and a little grated nutmeg.

Roll out the dough on a floured surface and use to line a 23-cm/9-in springform

cake tin or an ordinary cake tin. Place the broccoli, ham and parsley in the pastry case. Pour the egg and cheese mixture evenly over the ingredients and sprinkle the rest of the grated cheese over the top.

Place immediately in the heated oven so that the pastry cannot become soft and soggy. Bake for 25 minutes, then reduce the temperature to very cool (110°C, 225°F, gas ¼) and bake for a further 25 minutes. After removing from the oven, let the flan stand for 10 minutes before cutting it into equal portions.

1 **Crushing the peanuts.** Place the nuts in a polythene bag and crush them with a rolling pin or heavy bottle until almost ground to a paste, or use a processor for grinding.

2 **Lining the tin.** Roll out the dough and use to line the tin. If liked, do this by cutting a round for the base and a strip for the side. Cut a thin strip to seal the join.

3 **Filling the flan.** Place the broccoli, ham and parsley in the flan case. Pour the egg mixture evenly over the mixture and then sprinkle with cheese.

Blinis with Caviar

Blinis can be served with caviar, soured cream and fresh butter as a main dish for four or as a starter or snack for eight. They are delicious on any occasion.

---

150 g/5 oz plain flour
15 g/½ oz fresh yeast
pinch sugar
4 tablespoons lukewarm water
8 eggs, separated
good pinch salt
50 g/2 oz buckwheat flour
(available in health food shops)
450 ml/¾ pint lukewarm milk
150 ml/¼ pint single cream
450 ml/¾ pint soured cream
225 g/8 oz butter
225–450 g/8 oz–1 lb caviar or
lumpfish roe

Resting time: 30 minutes
Preparation time: 45 minutes

Making sure the plain flour is at room temperature, sift it into a bowl. Make a hollow in the middle, crumble the yeast into it and sprinkle over the sugar. Pour the lukewarm water over the yeast and sugar and cream them together. Mix in a little flour to make a batter. Cover the bowl and leave in a warm place for 15 minutes. Meanwhile, separate the eggs. Beat the egg yolks with the salt until creamy.

When the batter has doubled in size and acquired a honeycombed appearance, add the buckwheat flour and beaten egg yolks. Stir all the flour and the egg yolks into the batter, then gradually add the warm milk. Cover the bowl again with a cloth and leave to rise in a warm place for 10–15 minutes.

Stir the single cream and 150 ml/¼ pint of the soured cream into the batter. Beat the egg whites until stiff peaks form and fold gently into the batter with a balloon whisk until everything is well blended. Do not beat.

Melt a little of the butter in a frying pan. Using a tablespoon, drop the batter into the pan to form pancakes about 7.5 cm/3 in in diameter. Cook until bubbles appear on the surface and the undersides are golden, then turn and lightly brown the other sides. Drain the blinis on kitchen paper, then place in a clean tea towel. Keep them warm in the oven turned to its lowest setting until all are ready.

Form the remaining butter into curls, or melt it. Place the remaining soured cream in a small serving dish. Serve the caviar in a bowl on a bed of ice-cubes or in a decorative dish. Stack the blinis on a heated serving plate and serve immediately with the caviar, soured cream and butter.

1 **Creaming the yeast.** Add the water to the yeast and sugar and cream them together. Mix in a little flour to make a pool of batter. Stand in a warm place for 15 minutes.

2 **Preparing the batter.** Add the buckwheat flour and the beaten egg yolks to the mixture in the bowl and stir in the lukewarm milk gradually until smooth.

3 **Folding in the egg whites.** Beat the egg whites to stiff peaks and fold carefully into the batter with a balloon whisk so that they combine well. Do not beat.

4 **Frying the blinis.** Melt some butter in a frying pan. Place the batter in the pan with a tablespoon to form pancakes about 7.5 cm/3 in in diameter and cook until golden.

Our tip

Smoked sturgeon or smoked salmon are often served instead of caviar with blinis in Russia. We have used American salmon caviar which is not as expensive as the genuine thing, but for general purposes lumpfish roe is a reasonable substitute and is more easily obtainable.

Sherried Eggs with Mangetouts

Sherried eggs look like fried eggs but are in fact cooked in spicy chicken stock. They taste particularly good with tender mangetout peas cooked in butter.

800 g/1¾ lb mangetout peas
salt
40 g/1½ oz butter
½ teaspoon lemon juice
freshly ground white pepper
grated nutmeg
6 tablespoons chicken stock
6 tablespoons dry sherry
good dash Worcestershire sauce
4 fresh eggs
handful leaves fresh chervil

Preparation time: 30 minutes

Prepare the peas by cutting off the stalks, pulling off any threads at the same time. Remove the tips of the pods, pulling off any threads on the other side as well. Rinse the prepared peas quickly in cold water and drain. Bring a large pan of salted water to the boil. Fill a large bowl with cold water and ice-cubes.

The peas must now be blanched so that they retain their fresh green colour. This is done by placing them, a handful at a time, in the fiercely boiling water for 2 minutes, then removing them and plunging them into the ice-cold water in the bowl. Remove them after a few seconds and place in a colander or sieve to drain.

Melt 25 g/1 oz of the butter in a saucepan and add the drained peas. Season to taste with the lemon juice, salt, pepper and a little grated nutmeg. Cover the pan and warm the pods through over a gentle heat. Shake the pan frequently so that they do not stick.

Meanwhile, heat the chicken stock in a frying pan with the remaining butter, the sherry and Worcestershire sauce. As soon as the stock begins to boil, break two eggs into it. Simmer for 4–5 minutes or until the egg whites are set. Remove them from the pan and keep hot while you cook the remaining eggs in the same way. The stock mixture should be boiling fiercely when the eggs are placed in the pan; however, the heat can be turned down once they are in so that the liquid does not evaporate. This would make the eggs hard and rubbery.

While the eggs are cooking, rinse the chervil under cold, running water, shake dry and chop.

Place the eggs on heated plates. Season the egg whites with a little salt and pepper and sprinkle a few drops of the hot stock mixture over them. Season the peas and place next to the eggs on the plates. Sprinkle with chopped chervil and serve immediately. New potatoes with butter or sauté potatoes go well with this dish.

1 **Preparing the peas.** Cut the stalk ends off the pea pods, pulling off any threads at the same time. Cut off the tips of the pods and remove any threads on the other side as well.

2 **Blanching the peas.** Cook the peas for 2 minutes in fiercely boiling salted water, then plunge into ice-cold water. In this way, they will retain their colour. Drain well.

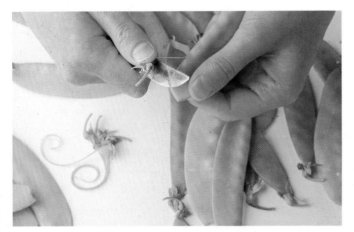

3 **Cooking the eggs.** As soon as the stock mixture is boiling, break two eggs into the liquid. Cook for 4–5 minutes or until the whites are set, then remove the eggs from the pan.

Our tip

You can compose dishes of your own using this recipe as a basis. Try cooking the eggs in seasoned chicken stock flavoured with white port or Madeira. You can use other vegetables as well, for example, blanched asparagus tips or tender young French beans cooked in butter. Lettuce strips, mushrooms or peeled, seeded tomatoes and herbs cooked in butter make wonderful alternatives. Whichever vegetable you use, do not overcook it. It should retain the 'bite' and freshness of the raw vegetable.

Poached Eggs in Dill and Mustard Sauce

Poached eggs in dill and mustard sauce turns a simple ingredient into a special supper dish. Serve with boiled potatoes and green salad or with toast.

---

about 4 litres/7 pints water
4 tablespoons white wine vinegar
1 shallot
1 bunch fresh dill
2 sprigs fresh parsley
$\frac{1}{4}$ lemon
8 fresh eggs
25 g/1 oz butter
1 teaspoon plain flour
1–2 tablespoons made mustard
6 tablespoons dry white wine
250 ml/8 fl oz double cream
salt
freshly ground white pepper
pinch sugar
Worcestershire sauce

Preparation time: 30–45 minutes

Even the most experienced cooks find poaching eggs to be a tricky business. It is made easier when really fresh eggs are used; eggs that are more than 5 or 6 days old are no longer suitable for poaching. When buying eggs, look for the week number on the egg box to find out when they were laid and packed. It is also important to have the ingredients prepared and ready before cooking the eggs to prevent them becoming dry or cold.

Place the water in a large saucepan so that it comes 5–7.5 cm/2–3 in up the sides. Add the vinegar and bring to the boil. It is necessary to have a large amount of water so that it does not cease boiling when the eggs are put in; this will prevent them sticking to the bottom.

While the water is coming to the boil, prepare the ingredients. Peel and finely chop the shallot. Rinse the herbs, shake them dry and chop very finely. Rinse and dry the lemon and grate the rind.

As soon as the water is boiling, switch off the heat, but leave the saucepan on the stove. Break one of the eggs into a cup. Take a ladle, dip it in the boiling water for a few seconds, then remove and slide the egg into it. Place the ladle on the surface of the water, then roll the egg over into the water so that the egg white closes round the yolk and the egg acquires a neat oval shape.

Repeat with three more eggs, then cover the pan and cook for about 3 minutes. Remove the eggs with a slotted spoon and place each for a second in cold water so that it does not continue to cook on the inside. Poached eggs are ready when the white is firm but the yolk still soft. To test if an egg is ready, remove from the water on the slotted spoon and press the egg yolk gently. If the eggs are overcooked, the yolks will be hard and rubbery. This can easily happen if the heat under the pan is too strong.

When the first four eggs have been cooked and are draining, bring the water to the boil again. Turn off the heat and poach the remaining eggs in the same fashion. When all the eggs are ready, take a sharp knife and trim off any loose or untidy pieces of egg white so that the eggs are neat and oval in appearance.

To make the sauce, melt the butter in a saucepan and fry the shallot until it is soft. Stir in the flour and cook for a few minutes, stirring all the time, until it begins to bubble. Stir in the mustard, then gradually add the wine and cream, stirring. Increase the heat and cook the sauce, stirring all the time, until it becomes thick and creamy. Season to taste with salt, pepper, sugar and Worcestershire sauce and stir in the grated lemon rind, parsley and dill.

Place the eggs in the sauce and cook very gently for 5 minutes. Baste the eggs frequently with the sauce so that they acquire some of its fragrance. The sauce must on no account simmer but just be kept warm over a very gentle heat. Serve hot.

If it is too difficult to poach more than two eggs at a time, warm them through again in hot salted water before placing them in the sauce. Eggs which have been poached and then placed for a moment in cold water will not start to cook through again. Another trick which helps make nicely shaped eggs is to make a whirlpool in the boiling water by stirring with a spoon and to slide the egg directly into the centre of the whirlpool.

1 **Sliding an egg into the ladle.** Break one egg into a cup. Dip the ladle in the saucepan of boiling water for a moment before sliding the egg into the ladle.

2 **Poaching the egg.** Place the ladle on the surface of the water, then roll the egg over into the water so that the egg white closes round the yolk.

3 **Trimming the eggs.** Take each egg and cut off any loose or untidy pieces of white with a sharp knife so that the egg acquires a neat oval shape.

4 **Place the eggs in the sauce** and heat for 5 minutes basting them frequently. Keep the sauce warm over a very gentle heat, and do not allow to simmer.

Deep-fried Eggs on Green Asparagus

Eggs deep fried in oil – what the French call 'oeufs frits' – puff up like fritters and create an interesting contrast for the palate between the crisp egg white on the outside and the soft yolk inside. They are particularly delicious served on a bed of asparagus pieces.

---

800 g/1¾ lb fresh asparagus
salt
40 g/1½ oz butter
freshly ground white pepper
lemon juice
about 250 ml/8 fl oz oil
4 very fresh eggs

Preparation time: 30 minutes

Rinse the asparagus carefully in cold water, paying particular attention to the tips as there may still be a little sand or dirt hidden in them. Drain. Trim the bases, cutting off any woody stems. Scrape each asparagus stem carefully with a sharp knife, working from the tip towards the base. Lay two or three asparagus pieces next to one another on a board and cut on a slant into 2 cm/¾ in lengths.

Bring plenty of salted water to the boil in a large saucepan and cook the asparagus for 1 minute. Place in a colander to drain. Heat the butter in a frying pan until it starts to bubble. Add the asparagus and cook, shaking the pan vigorously to prevent it from sticking, until just tender. Season to taste with salt, pepper and lemon juice. Keep warm until the eggs are ready.

Pour the oil into a small, deep frying pan – the oil should be about 2 cm/¾ in deep – and heat it. Test the heat by putting a small cube of bread into the oil; when it turns brown immediately, the oil is at the correct temperature. Now tilt the pan slightly and slide in an egg. It is advisable to wear oven gloves during this process as the fat tends to spit. As soon as the egg is in the pan, fold the white over the yolk with a spoon so that the yolk is completely enveloped and cannot become hard or stick to the pan. Baste the egg with oil frequently so that the white becomes crisp and brown. Remove from

the pan with a slotted spoon and place on a thick layer of kitchen paper to drain. Fry the remaining eggs quickly in the same manner.

Make a bed of asparagus on four heated plates and place an egg in the middle of each one. Season with a little salt and pepper and serve immediately, with fresh white bread or creamed potatoes.

1 **Sauté the asparagus.** Heat the butter in a frying pan until it begins to bubble. Add the asparagus and sauté quickly until just tender, shaking the pan to prevent sticking.

2 **Folding over the egg white.** As soon as the egg is in the pan of oil, fold the white over the yolk with a spoon so that the yolk is completely enveloped.

3 **Frying the egg.** Baste the egg frequently with the hot oil so that the white becomes crisp and brown. Remove with a slotted spoon and drain on kitchen paper.

Fish Twists with Prawns

Fish twists with prawns look like small works of art. The secret lies in buying really fresh fish; the twists form by themselves during the cooking process.

---

2 large sole or plaice, each weighing
about 450 g/1 lb, cleaned
250 ml/8 fl oz water
250 ml/8 fl oz dry white wine
1 onion
3 sprigs fresh parsley
1 leek
1 stick celery
1 carrot
salt
freshly ground white pepper
juice $\frac{1}{4}$ lemon
150 g/5 oz cooked peeled prawns
1–2 tablespoons dry vermouth
2 egg yolks
40 g/1$\frac{1}{2}$ oz butter
2 sprigs fresh dill

Preparation time: 1 hour

Ask the fishmonger to fillet the fish but to give you the bones and trimmings. Rinse the bones and trimmings in cold water, place in a medium-sized saucepan and add the water and wine. The liquid should cover the bones and trimmings. Peel the onion. Rinse the parsley and shake dry. Trim the leek and celery. Peel the carrot. Chop the vegetables and parsley coarsely and place in the saucepan. Bring to the boil, then reduce to a simmer and cook gently for 15 minutes, occasionally skimming off any scum which forms on the surface.

Meanwhile, rinse the fish fillets under cold runing water and pat dry. Lay the fillets on a wooden board and cut them in half lengthways following the grain of the flesh which narrows at the tail. Season to taste on both sides with salt, pepper and lemon juice.

Strain the stock through a fine sieve or paper coffee filter and return to the saucepan. Bring to the boil again. Reduce the heat and place the prawns in the stock. Cook for 1–2 minutes to warm through. Remove with a slotted spoon, place on a large plate with a little of the hot stock and keep warm.

Heat the stock again until it is boiling fiercely, then remove from the stove (do not switch off the heat). Place a few fillet strips in the stock. The fillets will cook through in about 1 minute during which time they will draw together into twists. Remove the fish twists with a slotted spoon and put on the plate with the prawns. Bring the stock to the boil again and repeat the process until all the fillet strips are cooked. Keep hot.

Bring the stock to the boil again over a fierce heat and boil rapidly in the open pan for 10 minutes or until the liquid has reduced to about 250 ml/8 fl oz. Season to taste with salt, pepper and the dry vermouth and remove the pan from the heat. Cool slightly, then mix 1 tablespoon of the stock with the beaten egg yolks. Strain the mixture through a sieve into the remaining stock, beating vigorously with a balloon whisk. Heat the sauce once again, whisking constantly, but do not allow it to boil. When it has thickened, remove from the heat. Chop the butter into small pieces and beat it into the sauce, a piece at a time.

Rinse the dill, shake it dry and chop coarsely. Drain any excess stock from the fish twists and prawns, then place on a heated serving plate. Pour over the hot sauce, garnish with dill and serve immediately.

1 **Dividing the fillets.** Place the fillets on a wooden board and divide each in half lengthways, following the grain of the flesh. Season with salt, pepper and lemon juice.

2 **Cooking the fish twists.** Place a few fillets in the hot stock and cook for 1 minute; they will draw together into twists during this brief cooking. Drain and keep hot.

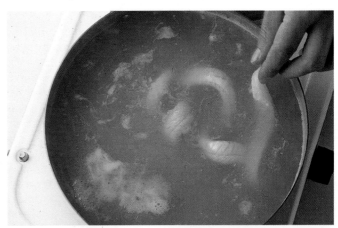

3 **Thickening the sauce.** Mix a little stock with the egg yolks, then strain the mixture through a sieve into the stock which should be hot but not boiling. Beat vigorously with a balloon whisk.

Our tip

Fish twists can be made from any kind of flat white fish as long as it is really fresh. Frozen fish is not suitable for this dish as the fish flesh no longer possesses enough tension to draw into twists while cooking.

Seafood in Butter Sauce

This exquisite dish requires spoons as well as fish knives and forks so that the delicate butter sauce can be enjoyed to the last drop.

---

4 large prawns
8 fresh or frozen scallops
8 fresh oysters
225 g/8 oz white fish fillets
1–2 boiled crabs or a little boiled lobster
2 shallots
6 tablespoons water
250 ml/8 fl oz dry white wine
(Sancerre, Chablis or Muscadet)
freshly ground white pepper
225 g/8 oz butter
small pinch salt
little dry vermouth or dry sherry
1 sprig fresh dill

Preparation time: 1½–2 hours

Peel the prawns, removing heads and tails. Cut the prawns in half lengthways and remove the black thread-like intestine which runs along the back. Rinse and pat dry. Pat the scallops dry with kitchen paper. Separate the coral from the white flesh. Chop the white flesh into two or three pieces. If using frozen scallops, allow them to thaw first.

If the oysters are still in their shells, open them as follows: lay the oysters on a folded tea towel with the flat side of the shell facing upwards. Grip each oyster firmly between the fold of the towel with one hand and open it with an oyster knife. This is done by firmly pressing the knife into the hinge of the shell and ramming it in horizontally. Force the two shell halves apart, running the flat side of the knife round the edges of the upper shell. Lift off the upper shell and remove the oyster from the bottom half, separating the muscle as you do so.

Cut the white fish fillet into bite-sized pieces. Remove the white crabmeat, or lobster meat, from the shells. Chop lobster meat into bite-sized pieces.

Peel the shallots and chop very finely. Place in a small saucepan with the water, wine and a little pepper. Bring to the boil and simmer for 5–10 minutes or until the shallot is soft. Remove the pan from the heat and cook the seafood gently in the hot stock in the following order: first the prawns and white fish fillet, then the white flesh (and coral, if liked) from the scallops, and then the oysters. If necessary, keep placing the pan on the heat again and bringing the stock to simmering point so that it is hot enough to cook the fish and shellfish in the short time. As a guide to cooking times: the prawns will need 2–3 minutes' cooking time, the white fish fillet 2–3 minutes, the scallops 1–2 minutes and the oysters 1 minute. When everything is ready, remove from the stock with a slotted spoon, put on a warm plate and sprinkle a little hot stock over. Cover and keep warm while the sauce is being made.

Boil down the stock over a fierce heat until reduced to about 6 tablespoons. Meanwhile, cut the butter into pieces. Beat one-quarter of the butter into the stock. As soon as the liquid begins to

bubble, remove the pan from the heat and beat in the rest of the butter a piece at a time. The sauce will gradually become white, creamy in texture and frothy. Season to taste with a very little salt and a little dry vermouth or sherry. Place the seafood in the sauce, garnish with the dill and serve immediately.

Our tip
The pieces of shallot can remain in the butter sauce if they are very finely chopped. If they are too big, strain the stock before or after reducing the liquid. Another way to make the butter sauce is to put the reduced stock into the blender goblet and to add the butter a piece at a time while processing. This must be done very quickly so that the sauce does not become cold.

1 **Halving the prawns.** Cut the prawns in half lengthways and remove the intestine which runs along the back like a black thread. Rinse and pat dry.

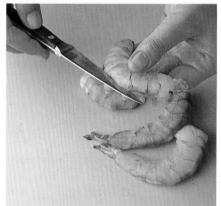

2 **Preparing the scallops.** Dry the scallops with kitchen paper and remove the coral. Cut the white flesh into two or three pieces. Allow frozen scallops to thaw first.

3 **Opening the oysters.** Press the tip of the knife into the hinge of the oyster shell and ram into the oyster horizontally. Force the shells apart and remove the oyster.

4 **Beating in the butter.** As soon as the liquid becomes frothy, remove the pan from the heat and whisk in the rest of the chopped butter until the sauce is creamy.

Paupiettes of Sole Stuffed with Prawns

Paupiettes of sole stuffed with prawns and mushrooms and served in a delicate creamy sauce make an excellent fish course for a special dinner.

8 sole fillets, each weighing 50 g/2 oz
salt
freshly ground white pepper
juice ½ lemon
100 g/4 oz button mushrooms
1 shallot
65 g/2½ oz butter
150 g/5 oz cooked peeled prawns
1 egg yolk
150 ml/¼ pint double cream
small bunch fresh lemon balm
butter for greasing dish
250 ml/8 fl oz dry white wine
(Chablis, Riesling or white
Burgundy)

Preparation time: 1 hour

Heat the oven to moderately hot (200°C, 400°F, gas 6). Pat the fillets dry with kitchen paper and season on both sides with a little salt, pepper and lemon juice.

Clean the mushrooms. Chop very finely and sprinkle with the rest of the lemon juice. Peel the shallot and chop very finely. Heat 15 g/½ oz of the butter in a frying pan and fry the mushrooms and shallot gently until they are soft. Remove from the pan and place in a bowl.

Chop the prawns very finely or reduce to a purée. Stir into the mushroom mixture together with the egg yolk and a few drops of the cream. Season to taste with salt and pepper. Rinse the lemon balm and shake dry. Put half the lemon balm aside, and chop the rest finely. Mix with the other ingredients in the bowl.

Dry the fillets again and place them, skin side upwards, on a working surface. Divide the filling evenly between the fillets and spread it evenly over them with a knife. Roll them up towards the tail.

Butter a casserole generously and arrange the fish rolls in it as closely as possible to prevent them unrolling. If the casserole is too large, tie the fillets with thread and remove it later before serving. Dot the fillets with 25 g/1 oz of the remaining butter. Pour the wine into the casserole from the side. Cover the dish with buttered greaseproof paper. Place in the heated oven and bake for 12–18 minutes or until the fish will flake easily when tested with a skewer.

Drain off the cooking liquid into a saucepan. Keep the fish rolls hot. Stir the cream into the liquid and boil down over a strong heat, stirring all the time, until the sauce is creamy in consistency. Season to taste with salt and pepper. Remove the pan from the heat. Chop the remaining butter into small pieces and beat it into the sauce, a piece at a time, with a balloon whisk. Cut three-quarters of the remaining lemon balm into strips and stir into the sauce. Leave the sauce to rest for 2 minutes so that the flavour of the herb is absorbed.

Place the fish rolls in a heated serving dish. Pour the sauce over and round the fish and serve immediately, garnished with the rest of the lemon balm leaves.

1 **Rolling up the fillets.** Spread the filling evenly over the fillets with a knife. Roll up the fillets, working towards the tail. Place in a casserole.

2 **Placing the paupiettes in the casserole.** Place the fish rolls as close to one another as possible so that they cannot unroll. Tie them with thread if necessary.

3 **Beating in the butter.** Remove the pan from the heat and beat in the remaining butter, a piece at a time, with a balloon whisk. Stir in the lemon balm strips.

Pike Quenelles in Cream and Basil Sauce

Pike quenelles in cream and basil sauce belong without doubt to the realms of haute cuisine. However, with patience and the very best ingredients, it is possible to master this recipe in your own kitchen.

---

1 pike, weighing about
1.25 kg/2½ lb, cleaned,
or other good firm fish
such as turbot, salmon,
sea bream, whiting or monk fish
salt
cayenne pepper
freshly ground white pepper
5 egg whites
750 ml/1¼ pints double cream
350 g/12 oz fish bones
and trimmings (preferably from
plaice or other white fish)
450 ml/¾ pint water
750 ml/1¼ pints dry white wine
1 onion
2 sprigs fresh parsley
1 small leek
1 stick celery
1 bay leaf
4 white peppercorns
1 tablespoon dry vermouth
1 egg yolk
1 bunch fresh basil

Chilling time: 1¾–2 hours
Preparation time: 1¾ hours

Ask the fishmonger to prepare and fillet the fish, but to give you the bones and trimmings. If any very small bones remain, remove them carefully before preparing the dish. The remaining flesh should weigh about 800 g/1¾ lb. Rinse the fish flesh under cold running water and dry thoroughly. Mince it as finely as possible twice or reduce to a purée in a blender or food processor. Season generously with salt, a little cayenne pepper and white pepper.

Beat the egg whites to stiff peaks and stir into the fish purée until it has been absorbed. The mixture should not be frothy, but a homogenous mass. Press the mixture through a fine sieve into a glass or metal bowl. Smooth over the surface and cover with a sheet of cling film, pressing it onto the mixture lightly with the finger-tips. Chill in the refrigerator for 1 hour.

Remove the cling film and place the dish on a bed of ice-cubes or in iced water in a larger bowl. Add 5 tablespoons of the cream to the fish mixture and stir until it has been absorbed. Repeat twice. When 15 tablespoons of the cream have been worked in, the mixture should be soft and creamy in texture. Place the bowl in the refrigerator again and chill for 15 minutes. The intensity of the seasoning will be lessened during the cooking process, so season the mixture generously. Return to the refrigerator.

Put 250 ml/8 fl oz of the remaining cream aside and whip the rest until it is slightly stiff. Divide into three portions. Fold each portion into the fish mixture separately. Place in the refrigerator again, and leave to chill while preparing the stock.

Rinse all the fish bones and trimmings and place in a saucepan with the water and wine. Bring to the boil slowly, skimming off any scum as it rises. Peel the onion. Rinse the parsley. Trim the leek and celery. Add all these to the stock together with the bay leaf and peppercorns. Cover and simmer gently for 20 minutes. Strain the stock. Put 250 ml/8 fl oz aside for the sauce and pour the rest into a wide saucepan. Bring back to the boil.

Remove the fish mixture from the refrigerator. To shape the quenelles, mould a little of the mixture between two tablespoons. Place a few quenelles at a time in the barely simmering stock and poach for 5–6 minutes. Put a little of the hot stock into another pan. As the quenelles are cooked, transfer them to the second pan with a slotted spoon, cover and keep warm. Before adding each batch of quenelles to be poached, bring the stock back to simmering point.

Place the stock reserved for the sauce and the remaining cream in a wide saucepan and bring to the boil. Season to taste with salt, pepper, cayenne pepper and dry vermouth. Remove the pan from the heat and allow the sauce to cool a little. Beat the egg yolk with a little of the sauce, then whisk into the remaining sauce in the pan. Heat gently, stirring, but on no account allow to boil.

Rinse the basil under cold running water, shake dry and chop roughly. Stir into the sauce and infuse for 1 minute, then add the drained quenelles and serve hot.

1 **Mincing the fish flesh.** Put the flesh twice through the finest mincing blade, or reduce it to a purée in portions in a blender or food processor.

2 **Passing the mixture through a sieve.** Press the mixture through a very fine sieve into a glass or metal bowl. Smooth over the surface of the mixture and cover.

3 **Adding the cream.** Pour in 5 tablespoons of the cream and stir until it has been thoroughly absorbed. Repeat twice, with 5 tablespoons of cream each time, then chill.

4 **Cook the quenelles.** Take a portion of the fish mixture and mould between two tablespoons. Place them one at a time in the simmering stock and let them cook for 5–6 minutes. Then lift them out and keep them warm.

Our tip

To produce light and airy pike quenelles, the mixture must be carefully made. Add the beaten egg whites and cream in small quantities and stir until the mixture becomes a uniform mass. Never beat the mixture, and keep to the times given in the recipe for chilling and resting the mixture.

Tuna Fish Provençale

Cook the sun-ripened vegetables, delicate herbs, garlic, olive oil and wine slowly with the tuna fish – the result will be an incomparable harmony of flavours.

1 large piece of tuna
from the tail, weighing
1–1.25 kg/2–2½ lb, or the same weight
in smaller tuna steaks
3–4 cloves garlic
8–10 anchovy fillets, canned in brine
salt
freshly ground black pepper
juice ½ lemon
2 green peppers
450 g/1 lb large, ripe but firm tomatoes
2 small courgettes
2 onions
1 bunch fresh parsley
2 sprigs fresh thyme
2 sprigs fresh oregano
1 sprig fresh savory (optional)
16–20 black olives
5–6 tablespoons olive oil
1 small bay leaf
6 tablespoons full-bodied
dry white wine

Preparation time: 2 hours

Heat the oven to hot (220°C, 425°F, gas 7). Rinse the fish and pat dry. Peel two or three of the cloves of garlic and cut lengthways into tiny slivers. Rinse the anchovies, pat dry and chop each one into two or three pieces. Using the tip of a very sharp pointed knife, push the garlic slivers and anchovy pieces into the fish between the concentric rings of fibrous tissue (not directly into the fish flesh). Arrange the garlic and anchovy evenly over the fish, on both sides. Season very lightly with salt (the anchovies are salty) and more generously with pepper, and sprinkle with lemon juice.

Prepare the peppers by halving them lengthways and removing the core and seeds. Rinse them under cold running water, then cut into strips. Scald the tomatoes in boiling water for 10 seconds, then peel and remove the core and any pieces of hard stem. Cut the tomatoes in half so that all seed chambers are visible and, taking half a tomato at a time in the palm of your hand, squeeze gently until the seeds fall out. Discard the seeds and cut the tomatoes into strips. Rinse the courgettes and trim off both ends. Quarter lengthways, then cut into 4 cm/1½ in pieces.

Peel and halve the onions and cut into strips. Rinse the herbs and shake dry. Chop the parsley; strip the leaves of thyme, oregano and savory from the stalks and chop the savory leaves. Peel and chop the remaining garlic clove. Halve the olives and remove the stones.

Pour 2 tablespoons of the olive oil into a large ovenproof dish. Arrange one-third of the onion, garlic and herbs on the bottom and sprinkle them with lemon juice. Place the tuna on the bed of vegetables. Arrange the peppers, tomatoes, courgettes and remaining herbs around and on top of the fish. Add the halved olives. Place the rest of the onion and garlic on top of the fish and sprinkle with salt and pepper. Crumble the bay leaf and sprinkle on top. Pour the rest of the olive oil over and around the fish. Pour the wine in from the side and shake the dish a little so that it is well distributed.

Cover the dish with a lid or foil and place in the middle of the heated oven. Cook for 1½ hours, basting occasionally with the liquid in the dish. Serve with French bread, or boiled or sauté potatoes.

Our tip

It is not always possible to obtain a large piece of fresh tuna fish as described in the recipe. Tuna steaks may be more readily available and can, of course, be used instead. The only difference lies in the cooking time: depending on the size of the steaks, the cooking time can be reduced by 15–20 minutes. If fresh tuna fish is not available, try the recipe with haddock, bream, hake or perch. Freshwater fish can be used as well, for example trout, tench, pike or freshwater bream. Whichever fish is used, it will acquire a new and delicious flavour from the herbs and vegetables.

1 **Inserting the garlic and anchovies.** Push the garlic slivers and pieces of anchovy between the concentric rings of tissue (not directly into the fish flesh) with the tip of a sharp knife.

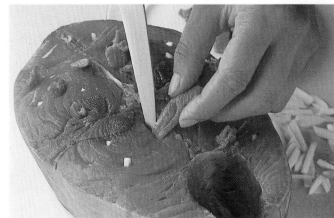

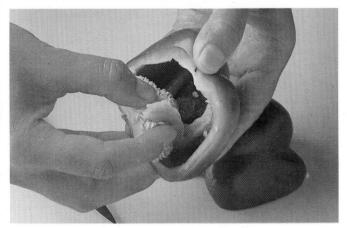

2 **Preparing the peppers.** Halve the peppers lengthways. Pull out the core and seeds with a quick twist, then rinse under cold running water to remove any remaining seeds.

3 **Adding the liquid.** Pour the rest of the olive oil over the fish and vegetables. Pour in the wine from the side of the dish and shake the dish to distribute the liquid evenly.

Mussels in Cream Sauce

Fresh mussels are available between September and April – in all the months which have an 'r' in them: a good reason for trying mussels in cream sauce.

4 kg/9 lb fresh mussels
1 small leek
2 sticks celery
1 bunch fresh parsley
small bunch fresh dill
1–2 sprigs fresh thyme
1 bay leaf
1–2 cloves garlic
40 g/1½ oz butter
freshly ground black pepper
250 ml/8 fl oz dry white wine
6 tablespoons water
1 onion
300 ml/½ pint single cream
1 egg yolk
salt
pinch sugar
pinch cayenne pepper

Preparation time: 1 hour

Scrub and clean the mussel shells thoroughly in several changes of cold water. Discard any which are already open. Remove the beards by holding them firmly between thumb and knife blade and scraping them off carefully. Place the mussels in a large saucepan.

Trim the leek and celery. Cut the leek into fine rings and the celery into thin slices. Put the leek in a sieve and rinse to remove any grit that might remain. Place the leek and celery on top of the mussels in the pan. Chop the parsley coarsely; pluck the dill and thyme apart. Place all the herbs with the bay leaf in the pan.

Peel the cloves of garlic and cut them into quarters lengthways. Place them on top of the mussels with a very small knob of the butter and a generous amount of freshly ground black pepper. Mix the wine and water and pour it into the pan. Cover and bring to the boil. Steam the mussels for 5–10 minutes, shaking the pan frequently so that all the mussels get an equal amount of heat to open.

Place a large sieve or colander over a bowl or pan and pour the mussels and the liquid into it. Strain the mussel liquid, which will have drained through into the bowl or pan, through a paper coffee filter or a fine sieve to remove any grains of sand and pieces of vegetable. Reserve the liquid. Remove the mussels from their shells, using empty mussel shells as tweezers. Discard any mussels which are still shut. Set the mussels aside.

Peel the onion and chop finely. Heat the rest of the butter in a saucepan and fry the onion until it is soft and golden. Stir in the reserved mussel liquid and cream, increase the heat and boil down the sauce until it is thick and creamy. Beat the egg yolk in a cup and stir in a little of the cream sauce. Remove the pan from the heat and stir in the egg mixture when the sauce is no longer simmering.

Place the mussels in the sauce, return the pan to a gentle heat and let the mussels warm through. The sauce should on no account be allowed to boil. Season to taste with salt, pepper, sugar and cayenne pepper. Sprinkle with the tiniest amount of cayenne pepper and serve immediately. Fresh French bread or black bread with butter go well with this dish. Serve the same wine as used in the sauce, or lager.

1 **Removing the beards.** The black strand known as a 'beard' must be removed. Hold it firmly between thumb and knife blade and scrape off carefully.

2 **Adding the liquid.** Mix the wine and the water and pour it over the mussels. Bring to the boil in the covered pan, then steam until the shells open.

3 **Draining the mussels.** Place a large colander or sieve over a pan or bowl and tip the mussels and the liquid into it. Allow the mussels to drain thoroughly.

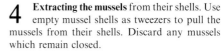

4 **Extracting the mussels** from their shells. Use empty mussel shells as tweezers to pull the mussels from their shells. Discard any mussels which remain closed.

Sea Bass in Puff Pastry

If you would like to serve something really unusual, try this delicious recipe for bass, stuffed with vegetables, herbs and prawns and baked whole in puff pastry. It requires time and patience, but is worth it.

Serves 6

---

1 bass, weighing 800 g–1 kg/1¾–2 lb
575 g/1¼ lb puff pastry, fresh or frozen
1 lemon
salt
freshly ground white pepper
2 sticks clery
1 small leek
1 sprig fresh thyme
2 sprigs fresh tarragon
1 bunch fresh parsley
25 g/1 oz butter
3 tablespoons dry white wine
2 hard-boiled eggs
100 g/4 oz cooked peeled prawns
3–4 tablespoons fresh breadcrumbs
2 eggs
pinch cayenne pepper

To thaw: 30 minutes
Preparation time: 2 hours

Ask your fishmonger to clean and scale the fish and remove the head, tail and fins. Rinse the fish thoroughly under cold running water and pat dry. If using frozen pastry, separate the sheets of pastry and place them on the working surface to thaw. Rinse the lemon in hot water, then dry well. Grate a little of the rind and squeeze out the juice. Sprinkle the fish inside and out with a little lemon juice and season with salt and pepper. Put on one side while you prepare the filling.

Trim the celery and leek and chop finely. Rinse the herbs, shake them dry and chop finely. Melt the butter in a small frying pan and fry the celery and leek over a moderate heat, stirring all the time, until they are tender. Add the wine and simmer until the liquid has evaporated. Remove the pan from the heat and allow to cool.

Shell the hard-boiled eggs and chop them. Chop the prawns coarsely. Mix the chopped eggs and prawns with the cooled vegetables. Add 2 tablespoons of the breadcrumbs, one of the eggs and the herbs, and season to taste with salt, pepper, cayenne pepper and grated lemon rind.

Heat the oven to moderately hot (200°C, 400°F, gas 6).

Place one-third of the pastry on a floured surface. Roll out into a rectangle that is large enough for the fish. Sprinkle the remaining breadcrumbs on the centre of the pastry in the shape of the fish.

Pat the fish dry once again and stuff with some of the prepared filling. Lay the fish on the pastry. Mould the rest of the filling into the shape of a fish head on the pastry. Trim off the excess pastry around the fish and 'head', leaving a margin about 2.5 cm/1 in wide. Separate the remaining egg and beat the white and yolk separately. Brush the pastry margin round the fish with egg white.

Take the next third of pastry, roll it out and place over the fish. Press this pastry lid carefully on to the base and seal the margins using a fork. Remove any excess pastry with a pastry cutter or knife. Using two large knives or spatulas, lift the pastry-wrapped fish on to a baking sheet which has been sprinkled with cold water.

Put the remaining third of pastry and the pastry trimmings on top of one another – do not knead them together – and roll out the pastry on a floured surface. Cut out small decorative rounds with a pastry cutter. Brush the fish all over with beaten egg yolk, then lay the pastry rounds on the fish to represent scales. Brush the pastry frequently with egg yolk so that the 'scales' stick on firmly. When it is ready, brush the fish with egg yolk for the last time.

Place the baking sheet in the middle of the heated oven and bake for 30–40 minutes. Remove from the oven and let stand for 10 minutes before serving.

1 **Shaping the fish.** Place the stuffed bass on the pastry and mould the rest of the filling into the shape of a fish head. Remove the excess pastry, leaving a margin.

2 **Trimming the edges.** Seal the margins together with a fork and remove the excess pastry. Lift the fish onto a baking sheet which has been sprinkled with cold water.

3 **Making the fish scales.** Place the pastry rounds on the fish to resemble fish scales. Brush the pastry frequently with beaten egg yolk so that the scales stick firmly.

Salmon Fillets in Tarragon Sauce

This beautiful dish of salmon fillets in creamy tarragon sauce deserves a place of honour on any special menu.

900 g/2 lb fresh salmon,
from the tail, in 2 fillets
juice ½ lemon
salt
1 onion
25 g/1 oz butter
4 tablespoons dry white wine
4 tablespoons dry vermouth
6 tablespoons double cream
4 sprigs fresh tarragon
5 tablespoons oil
freshly ground white pepper

For the stock:
350 g/12 oz fish bones
and trimmings
300 ml/½ pint water
1 onion
3 sprigs fresh parsley
1 small sprig fresh thyme
1 teaspoon lemon juice
6 tablespoons dry white wine
½ bay leaf

Preparation time: 1 hour

Rinse the fish bones and trimmings under cold running water and place in a saucepan. Cover with the water and bring to the boil, skimming off any scum which rises to the surface.

Meanwhile, peel the onion and chop finely. Rinse the parsley and thyme and shake dry. Add the onion and herbs to the fish stock together with the lemon juice, white wine and bay leaf. Simmer over a gentle heat for 15–20 minutes, then strain through a fine sieve or paper coffee filter.

To prepare the salmon, lay the two pieces on a wooden board and slice them both in half horizontally with a very sharp knife to make four flat pieces of equal size. Sprinkle both sides of the fish with lemon juice and salt. Place each slice of salmon between two sheets of oiled greaseproof paper and pat gently with the flat side of a carving knife to flatten. Set aside.

Peel the onion and chop finely. Melt the butter in a saucepan and fry the onion gently until it is soft and golden. Add the strained fish stock, white wine and dry vermouth. Bring to the boil, then strain through a sieve and return to the pan.

Pour the cream into the strained liquid, stirring all the time, then bring back to the boil and boil briskly to reduce until the sauce is creamy in consistency. Rinse the tarragon, shake dry and cut half of the leaves into thin strips. Place the strips in the sauce. Keep the sauce warm (but do not allow to boil).

Heat the oil in a frying pan and fry each slice of salmon on both sides for 30 seconds. Place for a moment on kitchen paper to drain off any excess oil, then season with a little pepper and serve with the sauce. Garnish with the remaining tarragon.

1 **Dividing the salmon.** Place the two pieces of fish on a wooden board and cut each in half horizontally with a very sharp knife. Season with lemon juice and salt.

2 **Flattening the slices.** Place each slice of fish between two sheets of oiled greaseproof paper. Pat gently with the side of a knife blade to flatten, but do not break the flesh.

3 **Reducing the sauce.** Pour in the cream, stirring constantly, and boil down the sauce in the open pan until it is creamy in consistency. Add the tarragon.

4 **Frying the salmon.** Heat the oil in a frying pan and fry the salmon for 30 seconds on each side. Remove from the pan and drain on kitchen paper.

Snails with Chablis Butter

Every gourmet will enjoy snails in Chablis butter. Serve them with French bread and the same wine as used in the recipe.

---

36 snail shells
36 canned snails
2–3 shallots
1–2 cloves garlic
150 g/5 oz butter
6 tablespoons Chablis or
other dry white wine
1 bunch fresh parsley
1 sprig fresh thyme
salt
freshly ground white pepper
Worcestershire sauce

Preparation time: 30 minutes

Heat the oven to hot (220°c, 425°F, gas 7). If necessary, rinse out the snail shells with boiling water and turn them upside down to dry. Drain the snails, reserving the liquid in the cans. Put a few drops of the reserved liquid into each snail shell followed by a snail. Press each one lightly into the shell so that there is still enough room for the Chablis butter.

Peel the shallots and garlic and chop them so finely that they are almost a pulp. Melt 15 g/½ oz of the butter in a small pan and add the shallots and garlic. Fry over a gentle heat, stirring constantly, until they are soft and transparent. As soon as the mixture starts to take on colour, add the rest of the liquid from the canned snails. Turn the heat up high, add the Chablis and let the liquid boil down until only about 2 tablespoons remain. Remove the pan from the heat and let cool.

Rinse the parsley and thyme, shake dry and chop as finely as possible. Beat the rest of the butter until it is pale and creamy, then mix in the cooled shallot mixture and the chopped herbs. Blend everything well together and season to taste with salt, pepper and a few drops of Worcestershire sauce so that the butter is piquant in flavour. Using a knife, seal the snails in the shells with the butter. All the snails should be generously covered with the butter. Press it well into the shells so that the snails really are enhanced by the flavour of the Chablis during cooking.

Arrange the snails on ovenproof snail dishes and place them in the heated oven. Bake them until the butter begins to foam up in the shells; they will then be really hot right through. Remove from the oven and serve immediately. Snails taste their best when they are served steaming hot.

1 **Filling the shells.** Put a few drops of the liquid from the cans of snails into each shell and then a snail. Press the snail lightly into the shell so that there is room for the Chablis butter.

2 **Reducing the liquid.** Add the rest of the liquid from the cans of snails, then stir in the Chablis. Boil until reduced to about 2 tablespoons of liquid. Allow to cool.

3 **Sealing the shells.** Using a knife, press the Chablis butter into each shell so that the snail inside is generously covered. Place the snails on ovenproof snail dishes and bake.

Our tip

If you do not have snail dishes, fill a casserole or baking dish with a layer of coarse salt about 2 cm/¾ in thick and stand the shells on it. Baked in this way, they will not fall over and can be brought to the table on the bed of salt.

Finnish Fish Pie

Surprise your friends with this unusual Finnish fish pie when you next invite them for an informal party. Traditionally, it should be served with a cool lager and an ice-cold aquavit.

Serves 8

---

425 g/15 oz light rye flour
200 g/7 oz strong plain flour
salt
450 ml/¾ pint water
215 g/7½ oz butter
2 trout, each weighing
225 g/8 oz, cleaned
2 small perch or herrings,
each weighing 225 g/8 oz, cleaned
450 g/1 lb fresh salmon
freshly ground black pepper
juice 1 lemon
450 g/1 lb lean belly pork

Preparation time: 1 hour
Baking time: about 2¼ hours

Sift the rye and wheat flours and 1 teaspoon salt into a large bowl. Make a hollow in the flour and pour in the water. Cut 65 g/2½ oz of the butter into small pieces and lay the pieces round the edges of the flour. Mix the ingredients together, stirring from the middle to the sides with a wooden spoon until the dough is very firm. When it is impossible to stir it any longer, remove from the bowl and knead and beat it with the hands until it is entirely smooth. Shape the dough into a ball and dust with flour. Return to the bowl and cover with a cloth. Set aside.

Heat the oven to moderately hot (200°C, 400°F, gas 6). Rinse the fish under cold running water and pat dry. Remove the head, tail and fins. Take out the backbone and any other large bones; the smaller ones will become soft during the long cooking process. (The Finns do not remove any bones.) Scale the salmon if necessary. Cut all the fish into strips about the thickness of a finger and season to taste with salt, pepper and lemon juice. Remove the rind from the belly pork. Cut the pork into equal-sized strips and season to taste with salt and pepper.

Knead the dough again. Dredge a sheet of aluminium foil with flour and place the dough on it. Roll it out into a large round about 1 cm/½ in thick. Place the seasoned fish and pork strips in layers in the middle of the dough round. Cut 25 g/1 oz of the remaining butter into pieces and dot over the filling. Using the foil to lift the dough, pull the edges up and wrap them over the filling. Release the foil and with wet hands smooth over the edges so that there are no gaps in the surface.

Line a baking sheet with foil. Melt the remaining butter and brush a little over the foil. Place the fish pie on the foil and shape it into a hemisphere with wet hands. Wet a knife and smooth over the surface so that it is quite even. Place the baking sheet on the bottom shelf of the heated oven and bake for 1 hour. Fold the foil over the pie to protect the surface and reduce the heat to moderate (180°C, 350°F, gas 4). Bake for a further 1½ hours. About 15 minutes before the end of the cooking time, remove the foil from the top of the pie and brush the pastry a few times with melted butter.

Remove the pie from the oven. Lay a piece of wet greaseproof paper over the top and cover it with a cloth so that the crust cannot become hard. The pie can be served immediately or allowed to cool and served warm or cold. To serve, cut a round lid in the top of the pie. Cut each person a portion of the crust, over which they should then pour some of the remaining melted butter and spoon a portion of the pie filling.

1 **Mixing the dough.** Stirring from the centre towards the edges, mix the dough together until it is very firm. When it becomes impossible to stir, knead it with your hands.

2 **Filling the pie.** Place the seasoned fish and pork strips in layers in the centre of the dough round. Dot with 25 g/1 oz of the remaining butter, cut into pieces.

3 **Smoothing the surface.** Pull the edges of the dough round up over the filling. Wet a knife and smooth over the surface of the pie. Bake on the bottom shelf of the oven.

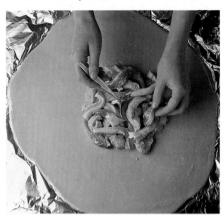

4 **Opening the pie.** Serve the pie hot, warm or cold. Cut a round lid in the top with a sharp knife and serve each person a portion of crust. Serve with the rest of the melted butter.

Liver Pâté

This recipe makes an excellent home-made pâté; you could not offer your guests anything more delicious.

Serves 8

800 g/1¾ lb calves' liver
350 g/12 oz fat belly of pork
2 shallots
1 clove garlic
2–3 anchovy fillets
1½ stale bread rolls
3 sprigs fresh thyme
2 sprigs fresh rosemary
1 sprig fresh sage
pinch ground allspice
pinch ground ginger
2 bay leaves
1 orange
2 tablespoons Cognac or port
1 egg
1 egg yolk
150 ml/¼ pint single cream
1½–2 teaspoons salt
1 (12.5-g/½-oz) can truffles
2 tablespoons green peppercorns
400 g/14 oz pork fat, thinly sliced or thin rashers streaky bacon

To marinate: 4–24 hours
Preparation time: 2 hours
To cool: 4–24 hours

Prepare the liver by removing any skin, tubes or sinews and cutting it into strips. Remove the rind from the belly of pork, then cut into strips of roughly the same size. Place the pork and liver strips in a large bowl.

Peel the shallots and garlic and chop finely. Cut the anchovy fillets in half. Remove the crust from the rolls thinly by grating it off. Cut the rolls into small cubes. Rinse the herbs and shake dry. Put a sprig of thyme and a sprig of rosemary aside for use later. Strip the leaves from the rest of the herbs and add them to the bowl together with the shallots, garlic, anchovy fillets and bread cubes. Season with allspice and ginger and place a bay leaf on top.

Rinse the orange in hot water and dry thoroughly. Grate the rind and squeeze the juice from one half. Sprinkle the grated rind and juice over the contents of the bowl and add the Cognac or port. Beat the egg, egg yolk and cream together, pour over the other ingredients and mix thoroughly. Cover the bowl with cling film or foil and leave to marinate in the refrigerator overnight or for at least 4 hours.

Heat the oven to moderate (160°C, 325°F, gas 3). Remove the bay leaf. Mince the ingredients as finely as possible, or place in portions in a blender or food processor and reduce to a purée. Return the mixture to the bowl and place on a bed of ice-cubes. Stir it with a wooden spoon until it is smooth and shiny. Season to taste with salt.

Drain the truffle, reserving the liquid from the can. Chop the truffle finely. Stir into the mixture together with the liquid from the can and the green peppercorns. Put the bowl in a cool place while preparing the terrine.

Line a large 1.25–1.5 litre/2½–2¾ pint terrine with about four-fifths of the pork fat or bacon rashers, arranging it so that a little hangs over the edges of the terrine. Turn the pâté mixture into the terrine and smooth the surface. Arrange the rest of the pork fat or bacon rashers on top. Place the rest of the herbs and the second bay leaf on the fat. Cover the terrine and stand it in a baking tin. Pour enough water into the tin to come halfway up the sides of the terrine. Place in the heated oven and cook for about 1 hour 10 minutes.

Take the terrine from the oven, remove the lid and leave it to cool. Weight the pâté overnight, if you like, but this is not really necessary.

1 **Marinating the ingredients.** Beat the egg, egg yolk and cream together, pour over the ingredients and mix thoroughly. Cover the dish and leave for at least 4 hours.

2 **Preparing the pâté mixture.** Place the minced or puréed mixture in a bowl and stand it on a bed of ice cubes. Stir the mixture with a wooden spoon until it is smooth and shiny.

3 **Seasoning the mixture.** Add salt to taste followed by the truffle, with the liquid from the can, and the green peppercorns. Keep çool while preparing the terrine.

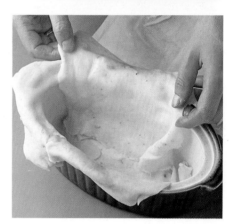

4 **Lining the terrine.** Line the terrine with about four-fifths of the fat or bacon so that a little hangs over the edge of the dish. Turn the mixture into the dish.

Our tip

The pâté will cut more easily if it is weighted after cooking. Lay a suitably sized board or plate on top of the pâté and use a large stone or a pan filled with water as a weight. Leave overnight before serving.

Saltimbocca alla Romana

This famous Italian dish – veal escalopes with fresh sage leaves and Parma ham – is well named. 'Saltimbocca' literally translated means 'jump in the mouth'.

---

8 veal escalopes, each
weighing about 75 g/3 oz
16 leaves fresh sage
freshly ground white pepper
8 thin slices Parma ham
or prosciutto
65 g/2½ oz butter
6 tablespoons dry white wine
salt

Preparation time: 25 minutes

Dry both sides of the veal escalopes with kitchen paper and place each one between two sheets of greaseproof paper on the work surface. Beat the escalopes with a meat mallet or rolling pin until they are twice as large as before and half as thick. Do not break the meat fibres. Remove the paper and press out any unevenness in the veal with the ball of the thumb.

Rinse the sage leaves under cold running water and dry very thoroughly on kitchen paper or a tea towel. Grind a little pepper over the escalopes and lay two sage leaves on top of each. Remove any excess fat from the Parma ham or prosciutto and lay a slice over the sage leaves on each escalope. Use wooden toothpicks to fasten the ham securely to the veal.

Melt 40–50 g/1½–2 oz of the butter in a large frying pan and fry the escalopes, two or three at a time, for about 3 minutes on each side. Fry the side with the ham last. Remove the escalopes from the frying pan as they are ready and keep warm. When all are cooked, pour the wine into the frying pan and loosen any meat sediments from the bottom and sides of the pan with a wooden spoon. Reduce the liquid by boiling rapidly until it is of a syrupy consistency. Season to taste with salt and pepper. Remove the pan from the heat.

Cut the rest of the butter into small pieces and beat them into the sauce, one piece at a time. Season the escalopes lightly on both sides with salt and pepper and remove the toothpicks. Place the escalopes on a heated serving dish and pour the sauce over them. Serve with French bread or a risotto.

1 **Flattening the escalopes.** Beat the escalopes between sheets of greaseproof paper until they are twice as large as before and half as thick, then press out any uneveness with the thumb.

2 **Covering the escalopes with ham.** Place a slice of ham on each seasoned escalope so that the sage leaves are covered. Secure with two wooden toothpicks.

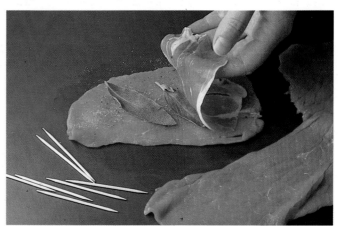

3 **Frying the saltimbocca.** Melt the butter in a frying pan and fry the escalopes for 3 minutes on each side, frying the ham side last. Remove from the pan and keep warm, while making the sauce.

Our tip

The type of ham used is important. It must be a mild, air-dried ham such as Parma or San Daniele. Smoked ham is far too strong in flavour and should not be used. The wine, however, can be varied. In Italy Marsala wine is often used instead of white wine and goes excellently with the veal.

Osso Buco

Osso buco – in English, braised knuckle of veal – is a typical Italian veal dish. Pasta, risotto with cheese or French bread go well with it – and, of course, wine!

2 onions
3 carrots
½ stick celery
3–4 cloves garlic
8 meaty knuckles of veal,
each weighing 225 g/8 oz
salt
freshly ground black pepper
50 g/2 oz plain flour
4–5 tablespoons olive oil
25 g/1 oz butter
6 tablespoons dry white wine
4 large ripe tomatoes
120–250 ml/4–8 fl oz
hot meat stock
small bunch fresh basil
2 sprigs fresh thyme
2 bunches fresh parsley
1 small bay leaf
½–1 lemon

Preparation time: 2 hours

Peel and finely chop the onions and carrots. Trim the celery, removing any hard strings, and cut lengthways into quarters and then across into very thin slices. Peel the garlic and chop finely. Heat the oven to moderate (180°C, 350°F, gas 4).

Wipe the meat with a damp cloth to remove any tiny pieces of bone. Season with salt and pepper, rubbing the seasoning into the surface of the meat. Tie up the pieces of knuckle firmly with heavy string. First bind the string round the pieces of knuckle, then tie them up like small parcels. Dust with the flour and press it lightly on to the meat. Heat the oil in a large frying pan. Add the pieces of knuckle, a few at a time, and brown on all sides. Remove from the heat.

Melt the butter in a large flameproof casserole and add the onions, carrots, celery and half the garlic. Fry the vegetables for 10–15 minutes or until they are soft and golden. Remove the casserole from the heat and place the well-browned veal knuckles on top of the vegetables.

Carefully pour off the excess fat from the frying pan, but retain the meat juices. Pour a little of the wine into the pan, stirring briskly to loosen any meat sediments, and bring to the boil. Boil to reduce the liquid to about half.

Meanwhile, scald the tomatoes in boiling water for 10 seconds, then peel and remove the core and any hard pieces of green stem. Cut the tomatoes in half so that all seed chambers are visible and, taking half a tomato at a time in the palm of your hand, squeeze gently until the seeds fall out. Discard these, chop the tomatoes and add to the casserole. Pour the liquid from the frying pan over the contents of the casserole and top up with the remaining wine and the stock. The meat and vegetables should be almost covered with liquid, so add more if necessary.

Rinse the basil, thyme and parsley in cold water and shake dry. Chop the thyme and basil finely. Place the chopped herbs together with half the parsley sprigs and the bay leaf in the casserole. Season generously with salt and pepper. Cover the casserole, place in the heated oven and cook for 1 hour to 1 hour 10 minutes.

To make the gremolata, chop the remaining parsley finely. Rinse the lemon with hot water, dry thoroughly and grate the rind. Mix the parsley and lemon rind with the rest of the finely chopped garlic.

When the meat is ready, remove the string. Discard the parsley sprigs and bay leaf. Serve the meat and vegetables with the gremolata sprinkled over it. The dish should be served straight from the oven or it will lose some of its flavour.

Our tip

In Italy knuckles of veal are served with 'riso giallo' – yellow rice – a risotto seasoned with saffron. The special rice called 'avorio' that the Italians use for risotto can be obtained in some delicatessens. It is prepared as follows: melt some butter in a pan and fry a peeled and diced onion in it. Add the rice and fry gently in the butter, then add small quantities of stock or wine as required until the rice is tender. Towards the end of cooking time, dissolve a tiny pinch of saffron powder in a little stock or water and stir it into the rice.

1 **Tying up the meat.** Tie a piece of heavy string round each seasoned veal knuckle so that they resemble small parcels. Dust with flour and press it on to the meat.

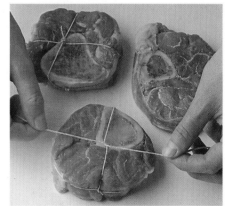

2 **Frying the ingredients.** Brown the meat well on all sides in the oil in a frying pan. Fry the vegetables and half the garlic in the butter in a flameproof casserole.

3 **Adding the wine and stock.** The ingredients should be almost covered with liquid. The amount of liquid required will depend on the size of the casserole.

4 **Making the gremolata.** Chop the remaining parsley finely, grate the lemon rind over it and mix with the rest of the finely chopped garlic. Sprinkle over the Osso Buco just before serving.

Vitello Tonnato

Italian cuisine is famous for its many delightful veal recipes. This braised veal dish with its spicy tuna fish sauce is one of the best and tastes particularly good on a warm summer evening.

---

1 joint boneless veal,
weighing 800 g/1¾ lb
(oyster or boned rolled leg)
1 onion
1 carrot
2 sticks celery, or ¼ celeriac
1 bunch fresh parsley
2 bay leaves
6 white peppercorns
150 ml/¼ pint dry white wine
450 ml/¾ pint chicken stock
1 can (about 150-g/5-oz)
tuna fish in oil
5 anchovy fillets
1 egg yolk
6 tablespoons olive oil
1 lemon
salt
freshly ground white pepper
2 tablespoons small capers

Preparation time: 1½ hours
Cooling time: 3–4 hours

Wipe the meat with a damp cloth and tie into shape, if necessary. Place in a saucepan which is just large enough to hold it so that it does not 'swim' when the liquid is added. Peel the onion and carrot and chop coarsely. Trim the celery, remove any tough threads and cut into slices, or peel and dice the celeriac. Rinse the parsley and shake it dry. Place the vegetables, bay leaves, peppercorns and three-quarters of the parsley in the pan with the meat.

Mix the wine with the chicken stock and pour it over the meat. Shake the pan to distribute the liquid and add sufficient cold water to cover the meat. Cover the pan and bring to the boil over a high heat. Reduce the heat and simmer gently for about 1 hour or until the veal is tender. Remove from the heat. Take out 150 ml/¼ pint of the stock for the sauce, strain it and set aside. Leave the veal to cool in the remaining stock. The cooling process will take 3–4 hours.

Drain the tuna and anchovy fillets reserving the oil from the cans. Place a small portion of tuna and two anchovy fillets in a mortar and pound to a pulp with the pestle. Pass the pulp through a fine sieve. Repeat with the remaining tuna and anchovy fillets. Set aside.

To make the thick mayonnaise base for the sauce, beat the egg yolk with a balloon whisk or fork until it is thick and frothy. Add the oil, drop by drop, beating all the time until the mayonnaise is thick and creamy. Cut the lemon in half and squeeze the juice from one half. Mix the juice with the fish pulp, a few drops of the reserved fish oil and a little of the reserved strained stock. Stir into the mayonnaise. Add enough of the remaining strained stock to give the sauce the consistency of single cream. Season to taste with salt and pepper and stir in the drained capers.

Remove the veal from the stock and drain well. Slice it thinly and arrange it on a serving plate so that the slices overlap one another. Pour the sauce over the meat. Slice the rest of the lemon and use as a garnish with the remaining parsley. Fresh white bread and dry white wine go well with this dish.

1 **Adding the liquid.** Pour the white wine and chicken stock over the meat and vegetables in the pan and add sufficient cold water to cover the meat. Cover the pan and bring to the boil.

2 **Pounding the fish.** Pound small quantities of tuna and anchovy to a smooth pulp in a mortar with a pestle, then pass through a fine sieve. Set the pulp aside.

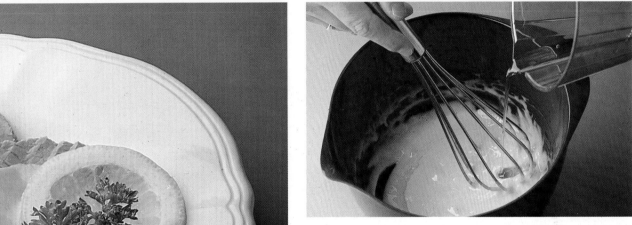

3 **Preparing the mayonnaise.** Beat the egg yolk until it is frothy. Add the oil drop by drop, continuing to beat until the mixture is thick and creamy. Add the remaining sauce ingredients.

Our tip

If there are any leftovers, they can be used to make other dishes. The meat can be cut into thin strips and mixed with diced cooked artichoke hearts. Serve on a bed of lettuce topped with any remaining tuna sauce. A few diced tomatoes make a colourful garnish. The veal could also be combined with pieces of celery, avocado · and chopped walnuts. Serve these ingredients with radicchio, fennel or lamb's lettuce to give the dish a summery freshness.

Fegato alla Veneziana

Calves' liver Venetian style is not a dish which can be made quickly; the onions need to be stewed slowly in butter and wine in order to develop the slightly sweet flavour which harmonises so well with fried liver.

575 g/1¼ lb calves' liver
300 g/11 oz onions
4 tablespoons olive oil
25 g/1 oz butter
1 bunch fresh parsley
6 tablespoons dry white wine
salt
freshly ground black pepper
little wine vinegar

Preparation time: 1 hour

Remove any skin from the liver by carefully lifting it up at the edge with a sharp knife and then pulling it off by hand. Hold the piece of liver firmly on the work surface with the other hand while carrying out this operation. Cut off any sinewy pieces and remove the tubes by cutting round them with a thin, sharp knife and pulling them out. The liver will not become hard and tough during frying if time and trouble is taken beforehand with the preparation. Cut the liver into slices 4–5 cm/1½–2 in thick, then cut these slices into strips about as thick as a finger. They should all be about the same size to ensure even cooking.

Peel the onions and slice thinly. Heat the oil and butter in a large frying pan and fry the onions gently, stirring them from time to time, until they are soft and transparent. Do not let them brown.

Meanwhile, rinse the parsley, shake it dry and chop finely.

When the onions just start to become golden in colour, add the wine and continue cooking as before, stirring frequently, until all the liquid has evaporated.

Increase the heat and push the onions to one side of the pan. Place the liver in the hot fat, a few strips at a time, and fry them quickly, turning frequently, until browned on all sides. Push those that are ready to the side of the pan before adding the next portion. When all are ready, mix the liver strips with the onions and season to taste with salt, pepper and a dash of wine vinegar. Stir in the chopped parsley and serve immediately as liver becomes hard and tough if it has to stand. Serve with fresh French bread or boiled rice.

Our tip

The dish can only be prepared as described in the recipe if you have a really large frying pan. If you do not, then it is better to prepare the onions in one frying pan and the liver in another so that the liver gets enough heat to fry through quickly. If you attempt the recipe using a small frying pan, the liver will stew rather than fry, and will become hard and tough.

1 **Removing the skin from the liver.** Carefully lift the skin with the point of a knife and then pull it off by hand. Cut off any sinewy pieces and tubes using a thin, sharp knife.

2 **Cutting the liver into strips.** Cut the liver into slices 4–5 cm/1½–2 in thick and the slices into strips about as wide as a finger. The strips must be of the same size to ensure even cooking.

3 **Frying the liver.** Push the onions to the side of the pan and place the liver, a few strips at a time, in the hot fat. Fry quickly until browned on all sides, turning frequently.

Calves' Kidneys in Cognac Sauce

Tender calves' kidneys in creamy Cognac sauce is a dish that is worth serving more often.

---

575 g/1¼ lb calves' kidneys
2 shallots
25 g/1 oz butter
1 tablespoon oil
2 tablespoons Cognac
3 tablespoons dry white wine
250 ml/8 fl oz double cream
salt
freshly ground black pepper
pinch sugar
small bunch fresh parsley
1 teaspoon green peppercorns

Preparation time: 30 minutes

Rinse the kidneys under cold running water, pat dry and halve lengthways. Clean the kidneys by removing any skin and fat and cutting out the cores. Do this carefully so that the kidneys keep their shape. Take a very sharp knife and cut the kidney halves carefully into slices 5 mm/¼ in thick. Dry the slices on kitchen paper. Peel and finely chop the shallots.

Heat the butter and oil in a frying pan and fry the kidney slices, a few at a time, for about 1 minute, stirring all the time. As each portion is ready, place in a sieve with a plate underneath to catch the juices.

When all the kidney pieces are ready, fry the shallot in the hot fat, stirring all the time, until it is soft and golden. Holding the shallot firmly in the pan with a spatula or spoon, pour off the excess fat. Add 1 tablespoon of Cognac and the wine to the pan and bring to the boil, scraping up any meat sediment sticking to the bottom and sides of the pan. Stir in the cream, and season to taste with salt, pepper and sugar. Boil down over a high heat until the sauce has reduced and is creamy in consistency.

Meanwhile, rinse the parsley, shake it dry and chop finely. Drain the liquid from the green peppercorns and crush them a little, if desired.

Remove the pan from the heat and stir in the juices from the kidneys, the parsley and peppercorns. Fold in the kidney slices. Return the pan to gentle heat and warm through. Do not boil or the kidneys will become hard and tough. Add the rest of the Cognac and serve immediately with a fresh green salad and boiled potatoes or boiled rice.

1 **Preparing the kidneys.** Halve the kidneys. Remove any skin or fat and cut out the cores, using a sharp knife. Do this carefully so that the kidneys keep their shape.

2 **Slicing the kidneys.** Using a sharp knife, cut each kidney half into slices about 5 mm/¼ in thick. Dry the slices on both sides on kitchen paper.

3 **Pouring off the fat.** Holding the fried shallot back firmly with a spatula, pour the excess fat from the frying pan. Add 1 tablespoon of the Cognac and the wine.

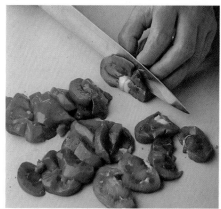

4 **Adding the kidneys.** When the sauce has been reduced sufficiently, add the kidneys and juices that have drained from them, the parsley and green peppercorns.

Our tip

It is not necessary to soak tender young calves' kidneys before cooking them. Only kidneys from mature animals require soaking, to remove their strong odour. It is very important not to boil the sauce again once the kidneys have been added. If it boils, the kidneys will be hard and tough and lose their delicate aroma.

Bitki Carnot

Russian cooks have often created really appetising delicacies out of so-called 'everyday dishes'. In the case of this recipe, meatballs (bitki) made from finely minced veal are stuffed with pâté de foie gras, coated thickly with béchamel sauce and breadcrumbs and deep fried.

---

65 g/2½ oz stale white bread
small bunch fresh parsley
450 g/1 lb minced veal
2 eggs
salt
freshly ground white pepper
1 teaspoon green peppercorns
1 can (about 75-g/3-oz)
pâté de foie gras
1.5 litres/2¾ pints veal
or beef stock
40 g/1½ oz cooked ham
1 small onion
25 g/1 oz butter
4 tablespoons plain flour
250 ml/8 fl oz hot milk
grated nutmeg
1 egg yolk
fat for deep frying
100 g/4 oz dry breadcrumbs

Preparation time: 1¼ hours
Cooling time: 2–3 hours

Remove the crusts from the bread. Tear the bread into pieces and place in a bowl. Cover with lukewarm water and leave to soak for 10 minutes. Meanwhile, rinse the parsley, shake it dry and chop finely.

Put the minced veal in a bowl and add the chopped parsley, one of the eggs, salt and pepper to taste and the drained green peppercorns. Squeeze the excess liquid from the bread, and add to the bowl. Mix the ingredients together well, kneading until the mixture is very smooth. Adjust the seasoning if necessary. Shape into balls about 4 cm/1½ in in diameter.

Make a small depression in the side of each meatball and place a suitably sized piece of pâté in it. Close the meat round the pâté and roll the meatball between the palms of your hands until it is smooth and round again.

Bring the stock to the boil in a large saucepan. When it is boiling, place a few meatballs in it. Reduce the heat and simmer for 5–8 minutes. Remove the meatballs with a slotted spoon. Bring the stock to the boil again and repeat the process until all the meatballs have been cooked. Drain them thoroughly and put aside to cool.

Dice the ham. Peel the onion and chop very finely. Melt the butter in a saucepan and fry the ham and the onion until they are soft. Sprinkle the flour over them and stir until the mixture becomes frothy. Gradually add the milk, stirring all the time, and simmer until the sauce resembles a thick paste. Season to taste with salt, pepper and nutmeg and remove from the heat. Beat a little of the sauce with the egg yolk in a cup, then stir into the remaining sauce in the pan. Leave to cool.

Heat the fat in a deep frying pan to 180°C/350°F. Place the breadcrumbs on a plate. Coat the meatballs thickly with the sauce, then roll in the breadcrumbs until they are completely and evenly covered. Set aside so that the breadcrumbs can dry on the surface.

Beat the remaining egg lightly in a shallow dish. Dip the meatballs in the beaten egg, then roll in the breadcrumbs again. Press the crumbs lightly on to the surface. Deep fry, a few meatballs at a time, in the hot fat for 4–6 minutes. Remove with a slotted spoon and drain on kitchen paper. Serve very hot.

1 **Filling the meatballs.** Make a small depression in the side of each meatball and fill with a piece of pâté. Close the meat round the pâté and roll into a smooth ball again.

2 **Cooking the meatballs.** When the stock is boiling, place the meatballs in it, a few at a time. Simmer for 5–8 minutes, then drain and allow to cool. Meanwhile make the sauce.

3 **Coating the meatballs.** Coat the meatballs thickly with sauce and roll in the breadcrumbs. Let the crumbs dry on the surface, then dip in beaten egg and roll in breadcrumbs again.

Our tip

Bitki carnot may also be served cold, but they must be thoroughly drained of fat after frying. Remove from the fat with a slotted spoon, let the fat drain off and then place on a thick layer of kitchen paper. Pat dry with another piece of kitchen paper.

Beef Wellington

Sufficient time for careful preparation is absolutely essential for the success of this version of filet de boeuf en croûte.

---

1 piece beef fillet,
weighing about 450 g/1 lb
2 tablespoons oil
salt
freshly ground black pepper
1 (368-g/13-oz) packet
frozen puff pastry
75 g/3 oz cooked ham
2 onions
1 clove garlic
1 carrot
1 leek
1 stick celery
225 g/8 oz button mushrooms
1 bunch fresh parsley
1 tomato
25 g/1 oz butter
4 tablespoons port or Madeira
good pinch dried rosemary
good pinch dried thyme
1 (75-g/3-oz) can
pâté de foie gras
2 tablespoons fresh breadcrumbs
1 egg
1 egg yolk

To thaw: 20 minutes
Preparation time: 2 hours

Pat the meat dry with kitchen paper. Heat the oil in a frying pan and brown the meat on all sides over a high heat for about 10 minutes. Remove from the pan. Season the meat on all sides with salt and pepper and put aside to cool.

While the meat is cooling, place the sheet of puff pastry on the work surface and leave it to thaw. Remove any fat from the ham. Peel the onions, garlic and carrot. Trim the leek and celery. Clean the mushrooms. Dice the ham and vegetables very finely. Rinse the parsley, shake it dry and chop finely. Scald the tomato in boiling water for 10 seconds, then peel and remove the core and any pieces of hard stem. Cut in half so that all seed chambers are visible and, taking half a tomato at a time in the palm of your hand, squeeze gently until the seeds fall out, then discard them. Chop the tomato flesh finely.

Melt the butter in the clean frying pan and fry the ham, shaking the pan all the time so that it does not brown. Add the prepared vegetables and cook, stirring constantly, until they are soft and any vegetable juices have evaporated. Stir in the port or Madeira and cook until the wine has evaporated. Turn the mixture into a bowl and leave to cool.

Add the herbs to the mixture with the pâté, breadcrumbs and whole egg. Season to taste with salt and pepper and stir until the mixture is well blended.

Roll out the sheet of puff pastry on a floured surface to a rectangle about 35 × 45 cm/14 × 18 in. Trim the edges, remov-

ing a reasonably wide strip with a knife or pastry cutter to use as decoration later. Set aside.

Spread about one-third of the vegetable mixture in the middle of the pastry rectangle and place the meat on top. Distribute the rest of the vegetable mixture over the meat so that it is covered on all sides. Press it on to the meat firmly with your hand so that it does not fall off later. Fold one of the longer sides of the pastry rectangle over the meat and brush with beaten egg yolk. Bring up the opposite side of the pastry rectangle and press firmly on to the first layer of pastry. Brush the top with beaten egg yolk. Flatten the two ends a little, fold them over the top and press on firmly. Brush all the edges with beaten egg yolk and make sure that they are firmly sealed.

Dampen a baking sheet with cold water. Place the pastry-wrapped meat on the baking sheet, seam and folds underneath. Brush with beaten egg yolk and arrange half the reserved pastry strips diagonally on top as a decoration. Brush with egg yolk again and lay the remaining strips over in a criss-cross pattern. Brush with beaten egg yolk for the last time and put to rest in a cool place for 15 minutes.

Heat the oven to moderately hot (200°C, 400°F, gas 6). Place the baking sheet on the bottom shelf of the heated oven and bake for 40 minutes. Open the oven door wide, switch off the oven and pull the beef close to the oven door. Let it rest in this position for about 10 minutes before serving.

1 **Covering the meat with the mixture.** Spread one-third of the mixture in the middle of the pastry rectangle and place the meat on top. Cover the meat with the rest of the mixture.

2 **Folding the pastry case.** Fold the longer sides over the meat first, brushing well with beaten egg yolk, then fold over the ends. Press to be sure all edges are firmly sealed.

3 **Decorating the parcel.** Place the pastry 'parcel', seam down, on the baking sheet, brush with beaten egg yolk and arrange the pastry strips on top in a cross-cross pattern.

Steak and Kidney Pie

Everybody enjoys a steak and kidney pie and this version with mushrooms and onions is especially tasty. Make sure that the puff pastry lid fits tightly to keep in the different flavours.

---

1 packet (368-g/13-oz)
frozen puff pastry
2 calf's kidneys,
each weighing 300 g/11 oz
225 g/8 oz beef fillet
or rump steak
100 g/4 oz button mushrooms
juice ½ lemon
1 large onion
small bunch fresh parsley
freshly ground black pepper
1½ tablespoons flour
2 tablespoons oil
25 g/1 oz butter
250 ml/8 fl oz hot beef stock
Worcestershire sauce
2 tablespoons dry sherry
salt
1 egg yolk

Thawing time: 30 minutes
Preparation time: 1 hour

Lay the frozen puff pastry on the work surface and leave it to thaw.

To prepare the kidneys, rinse them under cold running water, pat dry and halve lengthways. Remove any skin and fat, and cut out the cores. Do this carefully so that the kidneys keep their shape. Using a very sharp knife, slice the kidney halves. Dry the slices on kitchen paper. Remove any fat or gristle from the beef and wipe it with a damp cloth. Cut into 2.5-cm/1-in cubes. Clean the mushrooms and cut into thin slices. Sprinkle them immediately with lemon juice to prevent discoloration. Peel and dice the onion. Rinse the parsley, shake dry and chop finely.

Place the steak and kidney in a bowl, season generously with pepper and sprinkle with the flour. Toss to coat the meat. Heat the oil and butter in a frying pan and brown the meat, in batches, over a high heat. Add more oil and butter if necessary. Remove the meat from the pan with a slotted spoon and place it in an ovenproof pie dish.

Add the mushrooms and onion to the fat in the frying pan and brown them lightly. Remove with a slotted spoon and place them on top of the meat in the dish. Sprinkle with the chopped parsley.

Pour the hot stock into the frying pan and bring to the boil, stirring to loosen any meat sediments in the pan. Season the stock with a dash of Worcestershire sauce, the sherry, and salt and pepper to taste and pour it over the contents in the dish.

Heat the oven to hot (220°C, 425°F, gas 7). Roll out the puff pastry on a floured surface into a rectangle 5–6 cm/2–2½ in larger than the diameter of the pie dish. Cut a strip 2 cm/¾ in wide from the two long sides of the pastry rectangle. Dust the rolling pin with flour and wrap the rest of the pastry loosely round it. Brush the rim of the dish with cold water and place the strips of pastry on it. Press the ends of the pastry strips lightly together. Unroll the large piece of pastry over the dish and press on firmly at the edges. Cut off any excess pastry with a sharp knife or kitchen scissors. Holding a fork diagonally to the rim of the dish, press the pastry lid on to the strip so that the two

are sealed together. Small pastry decorations for the lid can be made from the excess pastry.

Prepare the lid by first cutting a hole in the middle, then brushing with beaten egg yolk and arranging the pastry decorations on top. Egg yolk holds the edges of pastry down so if you wish the decorations to rise properly, brush only the tops with egg yolk but not the edges.

Place the pie in the heated oven on the second shelf from the bottom. Bake for 20 minutes, then reduce the temperature to moderate (180°C, 350°F, gas 4) and bake for a further 20 minutes. Cover the pastry if it becomes too brown. Serve hot.

1 **Putting on the pastry strips.** Brush the rim of the dish with cold water. Place the strips of puff pastry on the rim and press the ends together lightly.

2 **Putting on the pastry lid.** Use the rolling pin to lay the pastry lid over the pie dish. Press the edges down firmly before trimming off the excess pastry.

3 **Knocking up the edges.** Hold a fork diagonally to the rim of the dish and press the pastry lid firmly to the strip. This will ensure a tight-fitting lid.

4 **Preparing the pie for the oven.** Cut a hole in the centre of the pastry lid, brush with beaten egg yolk and place any pastry decorations on top. Brush the tops with egg yolk.

Tournedos Filled with Pâté

Tournedos filled with liver pâté and green peppercorns and served with a sauce made from fresh mushrooms and cream are a special delicacy.

8 tournedos of beef, each
weighing about 75 g/3 oz
75 g/3 oz button mushrooms
1 shallot
small bunch fresh parsley
40 g/1½ oz butter
6 tablespoons dry white wine
salt
freshly ground black pepper
50 g/2 oz good quality
liver pâté
1 teaspoon green peppercorns
4 thin slices pork fat or
rashers streaky bacon
2 tablespoons oil
2 tablespoons brandy
6 tablespoons double cream

Preparation time: 30 minutes

Wipe the tournedos with a damp cloth and pat dry. Press the tournedos gently into a neat round shape using the ball of the thumb. Clean the mushrooms and chop finely. Peel and finely chop the shallot. Rinse the parsley, shake it dry and chop very finely.

Melt 15 g/½ oz of the butter in a small pan and fry the shallot gently until it is soft. Add the mushrooms and fry, stirring all the time, until any juices have evaporated. Stir in the parsley and 2 tablespoons of the wine, and season to taste with salt and pepper. Cook until the liquid has evaporated. Remove from the heat and put aside to cool.

Mash the liver pâté and mix it with the drained green peppercorns and 2 tablespoons of the mushroom mixture. Divide the mixture between four of the tournedos, spreading it evenly over the surface with a spoon or knife. Place the four remaining tournedos on top of the filling and press together lightly. Wrap a slice of fat or a rasher of bacon around the sandwiched tournedos and tie firmly with string. Cut the string just behind the knot.

Heat the oil with 15 g/½ oz of the remaining butter in a frying pan and sauté the tournedos for 2-3 minutes on each side. If you wish the tournedos to be well done, allow an extra minute or two. Remove the tournedos from the pan and keep warm. Pour away the fat in which they were fried and melt the rest of the butter in the frying pan. Add the remaining mushroom mixture and heat through. Stir in the brandy and the remaining wine. Bring to the boil, then stir in the cream. Simmer, stirring constantly, until reduced to a creamy consistency. Season to taste with salt and pepper.

Remove the string from the tournedos and place on a heated serving dish with or without the fat or bacon. Pour the sauce round them and serve immediately. Potato straws or Swiss fried potatoes and French beans or spinach with butter go well with this dish.

1 **Filling the tournedos.** Divide the liver pâté mixture between the four tournedos, spread evenly with a spoon or knife and place the remaining tournedos on top.

2 **Barding the tournedos.** Wrap the slices of pork fat or bacon rashers round the tournedos, press it into place and tie securely with string. Cut the string just behind the knot.

3 **Preparing the sauce.** As soon as the mushroom and wine mixture is boiling fiercely, stir in the cream. Boil down, stirring all the time, until reduced to a creamy consistency.

Our tip

If you wish to make this fine dish even finer, use pâté de foie gras, and add a finely chopped truffle to it. If you prefer a more rustic flavour, prepare it as described in the recipe but add a little crushed garlic and chopped fresh marjoram or sage to the mushrooms during the first stage of cooking.

Boeuf à la Mode

It is worth taking the time to try this delicious French recipe.

Serves 6

---

225 g/8 oz pork fat
2 small bay leaves
dried thyme
salt
freshly ground black pepper
4 tablespoons brandy
1 bunch fresh parsley
3–4 cloves garlic
1 joint beef silverside
or topside, weighing about
1 kg/2 lb
350 ml/12 fl oz
full-bodied dry white wine
2 onions
2 carrots
2 calf's feet or pig's trotters
50 g/2 oz fresh pork rind
2 tablespoons lard
350–500 ml/12–16 fl oz
strong veal or beef stock
350 g/12 oz small young carrots
150 g/5 oz small onions
25 g/1 oz butter

To marinate and cool: 5¼ hours
Preparation time: 3–3½ hours

Cut the pork fat into strips as long and as thin as pencils and put them on a plate. Grind half a bay leaf with a pinch of thyme in a mortar with a pestle and mix with some salt and pepper. Sprinkle the seasoning mixture over the pork fat strips (called lardoons), then pour over 1½ tablespoons of the brandy. Cover with a plate and chill for 30 minutes.

Rinse the parsley and shake dry. Finely chop one-quarter of the parsley, and set aside the remainder. Peel and very finely chop one clove of garlic. Mix the parsley with the garlic, sprinkle over the lardoons and turn to coat them. In this way they acquire an aroma which will seep through the meat later during cooking.

To prepare the meat for larding, use a thin sharpening steel to penetrate right through the meat parallel to the grain. Thread the lardoons into a larding needle and pull them through the holes made by the sharpening steel. Tie the meat joint into a neat shape if necessary and place in a deep bowl which is not very much bigger than the meat itself. Pour the wine and the remaining brandy over the meat and add the remaining bay leaves. Peel the 2 onions, 2 carrots and the remaining cloves of garlic and chop coarsely. Place round the meat in the bowl. Cover the bowl and put it in a cool place (not the refrigerator) for 5 hours to marinate. Turn the meat frequently.

Heat the oven to cool (150°C, 300°F, gas 2). Rinse the calf's feet or pig's trotters and pork rind. Place them in a saucepan, cover with cold water and bring to the boil. Boil for 5 minutes, then drain and rinse under cold water. Chop into pieces.

Heat the lard in a large flameproof casserole. Remove the meat from the marinade and dry well with kitchen paper. Place in the hot fat and brown well on all sides. Remove the chopped carrots, onions and garlic from the bowl, pat dry and place in the fat. Fry, turning, until golden. Add the pieces of calf's feet or pig's trotters, the pork rind and the rest of the parsley. Season to taste with salt, pepper and thyme. Strain the marinade from the bowl into the casserole. Add enough stock to cover the meat. Cover the casserole tightly and place in the heated oven. Cook for 2½–3 hours.

Thirty minutes before the end of the cooking time, prepare the young carrots and small onions. Scrape the carrots, and peel the onions. Melt the butter in a frying pan and turn the vegetables in it until they begin to take on colour. Add a very little stock to prevent them from burning and cook over a gentle heat until tender. Season to taste with salt and pepper.

Remove the meat from the casserole and keep warm. Strain the stock and skim off all the fat. Return to the casserole and boil the stock to reduce it a little. Slice the meat and arrange it on a heated serving dish with the young carrots and onions all round. Pour a little of the stock over the vegetables and serve the rest separately.

1 **Seasoning the lardoons.** Sprinkle the lardoons with the mixture of bay leaf, thyme, salt and pepper, and pour the brandy over them. Cover and chill for 30 minutes.

2 **Preparing the meat for larding.** Turn the lardoons in the mixture of parsley and garlic. Pierce right through the meat parallel to the grain with a thin sharpening steel.

3 **Larding the meat.** Pull the seasoned lardoons through the meat with a larding needle. Tie the meat joint into a neat shape if necessary, then marinate.

4 **Straining the marinade.** As soon as the meat and vegetables are well coloured, strain the marinade through a sieve into the casserole. Add enough stock to cover the meat.

Our tip

Ask your butcher to cut you a suitable joint from the muscle of the animal as the meat must be larded parallel to the grain of the meat. The meat from the calf's feet or pig's trotters and the pork rind can be served with the meat, if desired.

Traditional Roast Beef

Large joints of tender beef, such as rib, sirloin or topside, are all suitable for roasting. The roast joint should be moist and juicy, never overcooked or dry, and Yorkshire pudding, roast potatoes, horseradish sauce and gravy made from the pan juices are the traditional accompaniments.

Whether the beef is rare, medium or well cooked depends on personal taste and the cooking time should be calculated according to the times given below. Allow 15 minutes per 450 g/1 lb if you want a rare roast, 20 minutes per 450 g/1 lb for a medium roast or 25 minutes per 450 g/1 lb for a well-cooked joint. A meat thermometer can also be used as a guide. Insert the theremometer into the thickest part of the joint before cooking, then check the temperature when you think the joint should be cooked. A reading of 60°c/140°F indicates that the joint is rare, 71°c/160°F means that the meat is medium and 76°c/170°F gives a well-done roast.

Place the joint in the roasting tin, fat side uppermost. If preferred, the excess fat from a boned rib roast may be trimmed off before cooking. Rub the fat with salt and dot with a little beef dripping. If roast potatoes are cooked with the meat, they should be cut into even-sized pieces, blanched in boiling salted water for 2–3 minutes, then arranged around the meat in the tin. Cook in a hot oven (220–230°C, 425–450°F, gas 7–8) for the first 15 minutes to seal the outside

of the joint. Reduce the oven temperature to moderate (180–190°C, 350–375°F, gas 4–5) and continue cooking for the calculated time. Baste the meat and potatoes frequently during cooking to prevent the surface from drying out.

Traditionally, roasting is a method of cooking meat on a rack above a pan so that the fat runs off the joint. The fat has to be scored to allow the dripping to run freely and keep the meat moist during cooking. The Yorkshire pudding is then cooked in the pan below the meat for the last 40–45 minutes roasting time.

For the Yorkshire pudding, sift 100 g/4 oz plain flour into a bowl with a generous pinch of salt. Make a well in the middle of the flour and add 2 eggs with a little milk taken from 300 ml/½ pint. Whisk or beat the eggs and milk together, gradually working in the flour from the sides and adding the last of the milk. Whisk or beat the batter until it is quite smooth, then stir in 2 tablespoons water and allow to stand for about 15 minutes.

Pour off most of the fat from the pan below the meat – reserve this for the gravy – or, remove a little of the fat from around the meat and pour it into a separate roasting tin. Return the tin to the oven until the fat is hot, then pour in the batter and cook with the meat for about 40–45 minutes.

To make gravy to accompany the meat, pour off most of the fat from the roasting tin, leaving just a thin covering in the bottom of the tin. Over low heat, and stirring continuously, add 1–3 table-

spoons plain flour to the tin. Cook, stirring the juices out of the corners, for a few minutes, then gradually pour in about 450 ml/¾ pint beef or vegetable stock. Bring to the boil, stirring continuously, and simmer for a few minutes. Stir the juices off the bottom of the tin to flavour the gravy. Add a little gravy browning if necessary.

Serve the meat on a large platter, surrounded by the potatoes and accompanied by the Yorkshire pudding. Pour the gravy into a warmed sauce boat and serve separately.

1 **Score the fat for traditional roasting.** Use a sharp knife and cut a criss-cross pattern in the fat. This will allow the dripping to run freely, and keep the meat moist during cooking.

2 **Preparing the Yorkshire pudding.** Sift the flour into a bowl, make a well in the centre and add the eggs. Mix to a smooth batter with the milk, using a balloon whisk.

3 **Roasting the meat.** Place the pudding batter in the tin under the meat, so that it will catch all the juices, and cook for 40–45 minutes or until golden and puffed up.

Beef Stroganoff

First-class dishes do not always require much preparation: Beef stroganoff is a good example which proves the point. It is quick and easy to prepare and should be brought to the table as quickly as possible when ready.

---

575 g/1¼ lb beef fillet
or rump steak
2 onions
65 g/2½ oz butter
5 tablespoons hot beef stock
1 tablespoon tomato purée
½ teaspoon made mustard
250 ml/8 fl oz soured cream
salt
freshly ground black pepper
wine vinegar or lemon juice

Preparation time: 30 minutes

Carefully remove any fat or gristle from wide and the slices into strips 1 cm (½ in) wide. The meat should on no account be cut too thin or it may become hard and tough while cooking. Peel the onions and chop finely.

Melt about 25 g/1 oz of the butter in a large heavy frying pan. Add a portion of the meat strips and brown on all sides over a moderate heat, stirring all the time. Remove the meat and place it in a sieve with a plate underneath to catch any meat juices. Continue frying the meat in portions, adding more butter to the pan as necessary. When all the meat has been browned, add the onions to the pan and fry until soft and golden. Pour in the hot stock and bring to the boil, stirring to loosen any meat sediments on the bottom and sides of the pan.

Add the tomato purée, mustard and soured cream and mix everything together well, stirring constantly. Season to taste with salt, pepper and a dash of wine vinegar or lemon juice. Add the meat strips with any meat juices which have dripped on to the plate. Quickly heat the meat through again, but do not let the sauce boil or the meat will become hard and tough and the soured cream may separate. Place on a heated serving dish and serve immediately.

A selection of vegetables cooked in butter (for example, peas, baby carrots, mushrooms or asparagus) or a plain green salad with boiled potatoes or rice go well with this dish.

1 **Cutting the beef into strips.** First trim any fat or gristle from the meat. Cut into slices 1 cm/½ in wide and the slices into strips 1 cm/½ in wide. Do not slice too thinly.

2 **Stirring in the soured cream.** As soon as the onion is soft and golden, add the stock followed by the tomato purée, mustard and soured cream. Season to taste with salt, pepper and vinegar or lemon juice.

3 **Adding the beef strips.** Place the beef strips and the meat juices in the sauce and mix together. Heat through once more, but do not allow to boil or the soured cream may separate.

Our tip

The classic recipe for beef stroganoff has been argued about for a long time. The experts agree only on three ingredients: beef steak, onions and soured cream. However, there are many variations. Some cooks add a few thinly sliced mushrooms to the onions, others add tiny strips of gherkin and/or season with a little paprika. There are also those who add potato or beetroot slices.

Paupiettes of Beef

Paupiettes of beef with interesting new fillings: on the left with courgette and tomato, in the middle with beetroot and tongue and on the right with egg and spinach. The preparation remains basically the same.

---

4 thin slices beef top rump,
each weighing 225 g/8 oz
1 onion
1 sprig fresh parsley
1 stick celery
1 leek
2 tablespoons oil
25 g/1 oz butter
450 ml/¾ pint hot beef stock
1 bay leaf
150 ml/¼ pint soured cream

*For the courgette and
tomato filling:*
1 large ripe tomato
2 cloves garlic
1 bunch fresh basil
2 sprigs fresh oregano
1 teaspoon olive oil
salt
freshly ground black pepper
4 very small courgettes
50 g/2 oz goat's milk
or other soft, crumbly cheese

Preparation time: 1½–2 hours

To make the filling, scald the tomato in boiling water for 10 seconds, then peel and remove the core and any pieces of hard stem. Cut in half so that all seed chambers are visible and, taking half a tomato at a time in the palm of your hand, squeeze gently until the seeds fall out, then discard them. Chop the tomato finely. Peel and crush the garlic. Rinse the herbs, shake them dry and chop finely. Heat the oil in a small pan and fry the tomato and garlic until it is a smooth purée. Season to taste with salt and pepper, stir in the chopped herbs and leave to cool. Rinse the courgettes, dry well and trim off the ends. Crumble the cheese finely.

Pat the beef slices dry and season with salt and pepper. Spread the tomato and garlic purée evenly over each slice of beef

and sprinkle with the cheese. Place one courgette on each slice and roll up tightly. Fasten the paupiettes by inserting wooden toothpicks or metal skewers through the two upper layers of meat, or tie them up with cotton thread.

Peel the onion. Rinse the parsley and shake dry. Trim the celery and leek. Chop everything coarsely.

Heat the oil and butter in a large heavy frying pan and brown the paupiettes well on all sides. Add the prepared vegetables and continue frying until they are golden brown. Add a little of the hot stock and stir well to loosen any meat sediment on the bottom of the pan. Let the stock boil down before adding the remaining stock. Season to taste with salt and pepper and add the bay leaf and chopped parsley. Reduce the heat and simmer gently for 1–1¼ hours or until the paupiettes are tender.

Remove the paupiettes from the pan and keep warm. Strain the stock and return to the pan. Boil down until well reduced, then stir in the soured cream and heat through gently. Remove the toothpicks or thread and serve the paupiettes with the sauce.

Beetroot and tongue filling: Season the beef slices and spread with German mustard. Mix together 225 g/8 oz cooked tongue, chopped, 1 small cooked beetroot, peeled and chopped, 1 apple, peeled, cored and chopped, and 1 onion, peeled and chopped. Spread over the mustard on the beef slices. Rinse and shake dry a few sprigs of fresh dill and chop finely. Sprinkle on top, then roll up the beef slices tightly. Proceed as described in the basic recipe.

Spinach and egg filling: Prepare 225 g/8 oz fresh spinach and blanch it in boiling water for 3 minutes. Drain and plunge into ice-cold water, then drain again. Peel and finely chop 1 onion and 1 clove of garlic and fry in 1 teaspoon olive oil until soft. Place the drained spinach in the pan and cook for a few minutes with the onion and garlic. Put aside to cool. When the filling has cooled, season to taste with salt, pepper and grated nutmeg and mix in 25 g/1 oz Parmesan cheese, grated, and

40 g/1½ oz Emmental cheese, grated. Divide the filling between the four slices of beef and place one shelled, hard-boiled egg on each slice. Roll up tightly and proceed as described in the basic recipe.

1 **Filling the paupiettes.** Season the beef slices with salt and pepper. Spread the tomato and garlic purée over the meat and sprinkle with the crumbled cheese.

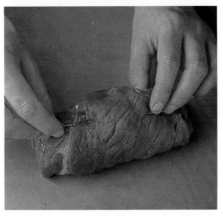

2 **Rolling up the beef.** Place a small courgette across a slice of beef at one end, fold the end over it and roll up tightly. Repeat with the remaining slices.

3 **Fastening the paupiettes.** Fasten each paupiette with a small metal skewer or wooden toothpick, which should be pushed through the two upper layers of meat.

4 **Adding the stock.** When the vegetables are golden brown, add a little hot stock and stir to loosen any meat sediments on the bottom of the pan. Boil down, then add the reamining stock.

Stuffed Belly of Pork

Stuffed belly of pork is just the right thing for those who enjoy a hearty meal. And it is an economical dish, too. A refreshing glass of lager makes a suitable liquid accompaniment.

---

1 piece lean boneless
belly of pork, with rind,
weighing 1 kg/2 lb
salt
freshly ground black pepper
1 tablespoon German mustard
2 leeks
1 stale bread roll
4 tablespoons hot milk
2 egg yolks
½ small red pepper
75–100 g/3–4 oz canned
sweetcorn kernels
450 ml/¾ pint hot meat stock
2 onions
1 carrot
1 stick celery
small bunch fresh parsley
1 large ripe tomato

Preparation time: 2¼ hours

Ask your butcher to cut a pocket in the meat which should almost go through to the other side. Pat the meat dry inside and out. Season with salt and pepper and spread the inside of the pocket with the mustard. Take a very sharp knife and score a criss-cross pattern in the rind without damaging the meat underneath. (If you prefer, this can be done after stuffing the meat.)

Heat the oven to hot (220°C, 425°F, gas 7). Prepare the leeks by trimming off the dark green leaves and the roots. Cut halfway into the upper, white part of the leeks lengthways, taking care not to cut the leeks in half. Rinse thoroughly under cold running water to remove any sand or dirt hidden between the leaves, and drain well. Blanch in boiling salted water for 3 minutes, then plunge into cold water. Drain and put aside to cool.

Chop the roll into pieces and place in a bowl with the hot milk. Leave to soften for 10 minutes, then squeeze out the excess milk. Place the bread in a bowl with the beaten egg yolks. Remove the core and seeds from the red pepper, and cut into 5 mm/¼ in dice. Add to the bowl

with the drained sweetcorn. Mix everything together thoroughly and season to taste with salt and pepper.

Press the sweetcorn mixture firmly into the pocket in the meat, then push in the two leeks so that they are both surrounded by the sweetcorn mixture. Sew up the pocket and place the meat, with the rind at the bottom, in a roasting tin. Pour over half the stock and place in the heated oven. Cook for 15 minutes.

Meanwhile, peel the onions and carrot. Trim the celery. Rinse the parsley and shake dry. Chop everything coarsely. Rinse the tomato, cut out the core and chop it coarsely.

Remove the roasting tin from the oven and turn the meat so that the rind is at the

top. Arrange the chopped vegetables and parsley round the meat and return to the oven. Reduce the heat to moderately hot (190°C, 375°F, gas 5). Cook for a further 1½ hours, adding a little stock from time to time so that the vegetables do not burn.

When the meat is ready, remove it from the tin and keep warm. Add the rest of the stock to the tin and stir well to loosen any meat sediments on the bottom. Bring to the boil, stirring. Skim off as much fat as possible, then strain the liquid through a sieve into a saucepan, pressing the vegetables through the fine mesh of the sieve with a spoon. Thicken the gravy by boiling it down. Season to taste with salt and pepper. After removing the thread, slice the meat and serve with the gravy.

1 **Preparing the leeks.** Remove the coarse dark green leaves and the roots, then cut open the upper half of the stem lengthways without cutting right through the leek. Rinse thoroughly.

2 **Stuffing the pork.** Fill the pocket with the sweetcorn mixture and push in the leeks through so that they are completely surrounded by the sweetcorn stuffing.

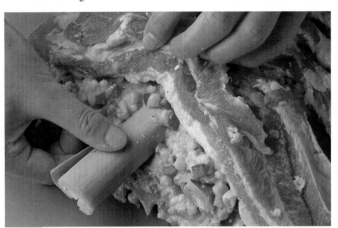

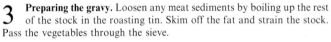

3 **Preparing the gravy.** Loosen any meat sediments by boiling up the rest of the stock in the roasting tin. Skim off the fat and strain the stock. Pass the vegetables through the sieve.

Roast Pork Danish Style

This roast, slowly cooked in wine and cream, is enhanced by a filling of sweet prunes, tart apples and aromatic herbs. It is a dish for those who appreciate hearty home cooking.

Serves 6

---

75 g/3 oz prunes
1 joint boneless loin of pork,
rind removed, weighing
800 g–1 kg/1¾–2 lb
salt
freshly ground black pepper
1 small cooking apple
juice ½ lemon
2 sprigs fresh marjoram
2 sprigs fresh thyme
2 tablespoons oil
25 g/1 oz butter
6 tablespoons full-bodied
dry white wine
300 ml/½ pint single cream
1–2 tablespoons redcurrant jelly

Soaking time (prunes): 30 minutes
Preparation time: 1¾ hours

Soak the prunes in hot water for 30 minutes. Meanwhile, wipe the meat with a damp cloth and pat dry. Score a cross in each end of the meat, then push a sharpening steel lengthways through the meat to make room for the filling. Season the opening with salt and pepper.

Peel, core and finely chop the apple. Sprinkle with the lemon juice to prevent discoloration. Rinse the herbs, shake dry and chop half of them. Drain the prunes and stone them. Mix the prunes with the apples and herbs and stuff this filling into the pork, using the handle of a wooden spoon to press it through.

Take a long piece of string and make a loop at one end. Pull the loop tightly round one end of the meat, pulling the other end of the string through and binding it round again and again. Secure it at the top so that the joint has the shape of a long narrow bolster. Season with salt and pepper. Heat the oven to moderate (180°C, 350°F, gas 4).

Heat the oil and butter in a roasting tin on top of the stove and sear the meat well

on all sides. This should take about 20 minutes. Remove the joint and carefully pour off any excess fat from the tin. Return the tin to the heat and pour in the wine, then add the cream, stirring vigorously all the time. Return the meat to the tin. Heat the liquid almost to boiling point. Season to taste with salt and pepper and add the rest of the herbs. Cover the tin and place in the heated oven. Roast for 1 hour.

Remove the meat from the tin when it is cooked and keep warm. Skim off any fat from the liquid and strain into a saucepan. Stir in the redcurrant jelly and boil down over a strong heat until the sauce

becomes creamy in consistency. Taste and adjust the seasoning.

Remove the string from the meat and cut into slices 1 cm/½ in thick. Serve the slices on a heated dish with a little of the sauce separately. Boiled potatoes, braised red cabbage or even a green salad go well with this dish. A dry white wine makes a good accompanying drink.

Our tip

You will find it even easier to stuff the pork if you cut a pocket in the meat. Begin about 2 cm/¾ in away from one end of the joint and cut a clean, deep slit, running the whole length of the joint stopping well short of cutting all the way through to the bottom. Leave another 2 cm/¾ in uncut at the opposite end of the meat as well so that the stuffing cannot fall out during cooking or turning the meat. Season the inside of the meat, fill it with the apple mixture and sew the opening tightly together again. Before carving and serving the meat you will of course have to remove all the threads.

1 **Preparing the pork.** Score a cross in each end of the meat, then push a sharpening steel through the meat to make a tunnel for the filling. Season the opening with salt and pepper.

2 **Stuffing the meat.** Push the apple, prune and herb mixture into the tunnel in the loin of pork and press it through with the handle of a wooden spoon.

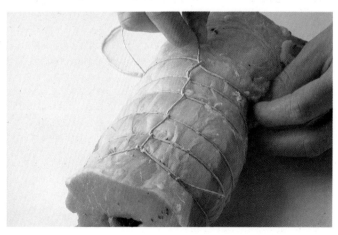

3 **Tying the meat.** Tie string around the meat, looping it as a butcher does. Secure it at the top and finish with a firm knot. Season the meat with salt and pepper.

Pork Fillet with Peas

Pork fillet with peas is a dish which has its origins in the Far East. Serve it Asian style, with a bowl of rice.

---

450 g/1 lb pork fillet
1 egg white
1 tablespoon cornflour
3 tablespoons soy sauce
4–5 tablespoons rice wine
or dry sherry
freshly ground black pepper
100 g/4 oz frozen peas
salt
1 leek
1 shallot
1 clove garlic
100 g/4 oz canned bamboo shoots
2 tablespoons sesame seeds
4 tablespoons oil
1 teaspoon green peppercorns
6 tablespoons hot chicken stock
pinch ground ginger (optional)

To marinate: 40 minutes
Preparation time: 30 minutes

Wipe the pork with a damp cloth and pat dry. Cut the meat into slices 5 mm/¼ in thick, cutting across or diagonally to the grain of the meat (this will depend on the thickness of the fillet). Halve the slices lengthways. Mix the egg white and cornflour together in a bowl. Add half the soy sauce, about 3 tablespoons of the rice wine or dry sherry and a little freshly ground pepper. Beat the ingredients together vigorously. Place the meat strips in the marinade, cover the bowl and leave in a cool place (not the refrigerator) for 40 minutes.

Meanwhile, cook the peas in boiling salted water as directed on the packet. Drain in a sieve, then rinse under cold running water to cool. Drain again and set aside. Trim the roots and dark green leaves from the leek. Cut it into pieces 4 cm/1½ in long, then cut these lengthways into strips 3 mm/⅛ in wide. Place the strips in a sieve under cold running water and rinse thoroughly to remove any grit that might remain. Put aside to drain. Peel the shallot and garlic. Dice the shallot and chop the garlic very finely. Drain the bamboo shoots and cut them into strips 3 mm/⅛ in wide.

When the meat has been in the marinade for 40 minutes, heat a wok or frying pan. When the pan is really hot, place the sesame seeds in it and toast them until they are golden in colour, stirring all the time so that they do not burn. Remove from the pan and set aside.

Heat a little of the oil in the pan. Add the meat strips, a few at a time, and fry briskly until browned on all sides. Remove from the pan and place in a sieve with a plate underneath to catch the meat juices. Add a little more oil to the pan when necessary. When all the meat has been browned, place the leek, shallot, garlic and bamboo shoots in the pan and stir-fry until they are glassy in appearance. Stir in the peas, green peppercorns and hot chicken stock and bring to the boil. Boil briskly for 1–2 minutes, or until the vegetables are just tender.

Return the meat to the pan, with any meat juices. Warm everything through again but do not boil. Add the rest of the soy sauce and rice wine or sherry, and season to taste with a little salt and/or ground ginger. Serve immediately, sprinkled with the sesame seeds, so that the vegetables lose nothing of their crisp freshness.

1 **Marinating the meat.** Place the strips of pork fillet in the marinade, cover and leave in a cool place for 40 minutes. Meanwhile, cook the peas as directed on the packet.

2 **Chopping the leek.** First cut the leek into 4 cm/1½ in lengths and then into strips 3 mm/⅛ in wide. Place in a sieve and rinse thoroughly under cold running water.

3 **Toasting the sesame seeds.** Place the seeds in a hot wok or frying pan, without fat. Toast them over a high heat, stirring constantly, until they are golden.

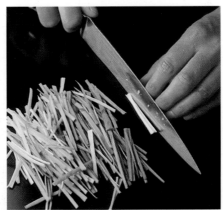

4 **Adding the meat.** As soon as the vegetables are just tender, return the pork to the pan with any meat juices. Heat through, but do not allow to boil.

Our tip

It is important to cook the pork quickly so that it remains tender. Fry small portions at a time and stir constantly so that the pork is seared on all sides as quickly as possible. Meat that begins to cook in its own juices becomes easily tough.

Marinated Leg of Lamb

Roast leg of lamb should be moist and juicy in the middle and is sometimes preferred as rare as in the photograph here.

4–6 cloves garlic
freshly ground black pepper
1–2 tablespoons Armagnac or Cognac
3 tablespoons olive oil
3 sprigs fresh rosemary
small bunch fresh thyme
2 bay leaves
1 leg of lamb, weighing
about 1 kg/2 lb
50 g/2 oz butter, softened
salt

To marinate: 12–24 hours
Preparation time: 1½ hours

Peel the cloves of garlic and chop very finely or crush in a garlic press. Sprinkle with freshly ground black pepper (about ½ teaspoon) and mix with the Armagnac or Cognac. Beat in the oil, drop by drop. Rinse the rosemary and thyme and shake dry. Strip the needle-like leaves from the rosemary and chop the thyme roughly. Spread a large piece of extra strong aluminium foil on the work surface and sprinkle a little of the rosemary and thyme in the middle. Crumble one of the bay leaves over the herbs.

Wipe the joint with a damp cloth and pat dry with kitchen paper. Brush the joint with the garlic and oil mixture and put it on top of the herbs on the foil. Sprinkle the remaining herbs over the joint. Wrap it tightly in foil so that none of the aroma of the seasonings can be lost. Place the lamb in a cool place and leave to marinate overnight or, even better, for 24 hours; a cool larder is better than the refrigerator. If you do not have a cool larder, the refrigerator can be used but the joint should be removed 2 hours before cooking since the aroma can develop better in the foil at room temperature.

When you are ready to cook the lamb, heat the oven to very hot (240°C, 475°F, gas 9). Unwrap the joint and carefully scrape off the herb and garlic mixture or wipe it off with kitchen paper. This is very important for if it is not completely removed, it will burn during cooking and taste bitter. Pat the lamb dry with kitchen paper. Brush two-thirds of the softened butter evenly over the joint, then season it on all sides with salt. If you are using a meat thermometer, insert it into the thickest part of the joint, making sure that the needle does not touch the bone.

Place the joint on an oven shelf over a roasting tin, or on a rack in a tin, in the heated oven. Reduce the temperature to moderately hot (200°C, 400°F, gas 6) and roast the meat for 45 minutes to 1 hour, or until the meat thermometer registers 82°C/180°F. Baste frequently with the remaining butter during this time.

Remove the joint from the oven and let it rest, loosely wrapped in foil, for 10–15 minutes. Slice the meat on a slant to the bone or grain of the meat and season again with salt and pepper if desired. Serve hot.

1 **Marinating the lamb.** Brush the joint all over with the garlic and oil mixture and place on top of the herbs on the foil. Distribute the remaining herbs over the joint and wrap tightly in foil.

2 **Brushing the joint with butter.** Scrape off the herbs and garlic mixture, then spread two-thirds of the softened butter over the joint. Season with salt. Reserve the rest of the butter for basting.

3 **Attaching the meat thermometer.** If you are using a meat thermometer, insert it into the thickest part of the meat. The needle should not touch the bone. Place the joint on an oven shelf over a roasting tin or on a roasting rack in a tin.

Crown Roast of Lamb with French Beans

Crown roast of lamb with French beans – tender, juicy and wonderfully fragrant – is not as difficult to make as it looks.

---

1 joint best end of neck, in a piece, weighing about 2 kg/4½ lb
1 sprig fresh rosemary
2 sprigs fresh thyme
3–4 cloves garlic
pinch dried sage
4 tablespoons olive oil
salt
freshly ground black pepper
25 g/1 oz butter · 1 onion
1 carrot · 1 stick celery
1 bunch fresh parsley
6 tablespoons full-bodied dry red wine
6 tablespoons hot meat stock
6 tablespoons double cream

For the garnish:
450 g/1 lb tender young French beans
salt · 1 onion
2 cloves garlic
2 large ripe tomatoes
1 bunch fresh basil
1 sprig fresh thyme
2 tablespoons olive oil

To marinate: 18–24 hours
Preparation time: 2 hours

Carefully remove any pieces of skin or sinew from the meat and trim back any thick layers of fat. Remove any small bone splinters with a damp cloth. Trim the ends of the bones by cutting off about 4 cm/1½ in of skin and the thin layer of meat which lies directly on the bone. Place the meat fat side down on the work surface.

In order to stretch the joint to make the crown, it is necessary to cut into the meat between every second cutlet and pull the bones apart a little. Bend the meat a little towards the inside while this is being done so that it is easier to shape and bind later. Form the crown by bending the joint round with the fat to the middle until both ends meet. Secure by inserting a wooden toothpick through the upper part of the meat. Once the crown has been formed and pinned together, it can be tied with string. Draw the string round the lower part of the joint, pull it tight and tie with a firm knot.

Rinse the rosemary and thyme, pat them dry and chop. Peel 2–3 cloves of garlic and chop them finely or crush with a little salt in a garlic press. Mix the garlic, rosemary, thyme, sage and 2 tablespoons of the oil to a paste. Rub the mixture over the joint, then wrap it in aluminium foil and leave to marinate for 18–24 hours.

About 1 hour before the lamb is to be served, heat the oven to hot (230°C, 450°F, gas 8). Unwrap the joint and scrape off the herb mixture. Season the joint with salt and pepper and brush it all over with 1 tablespoon of the remaining oil. Heat the rest of the oil and the butter in a flat roasting tin. Place the joint in the fat and put the tin on the bottom shelf of the heated oven. Roast for 15 minutes.

Meanwhile, peel the remaining garlic, the onion and carrot. Trim the celery. Chop everything coarsely. Rinse the parsley, shake it dry and chop. When the meat has been in the oven for 15 minutes, place the vegetables and herbs in the roasting tin around the joint and let them go nicely brown in the hot fat. Continue roasting for about 30 minutes. Mix the wine and stock together and add just enough liquid to the tin from time to time to prevent the herbs and vegetables from burning.

Remove the joint when it is ready and wrap it loosely in foil. Put it to rest in a warm place for 15 minutes. Pour the rest of the wine and stock mixture into the tin and bring to the boil on top of the stove, stirring to loosen any meat sediments in the tin. Strain the liquid into a saucepan. Stir in the cream and boil rapidly to reduce to a creamy gravy. Keep warm.

To prepare the beans, trim, and break into pieces about 4 cm/1½ in in length. Cook in boiling salted water for 8 minutes. Place in a sieve and rinse under cold water to cool. Put aside to drain.

Peel the onion and slice into rings. Peel and crush the garlic. Scald the tomatoes in boiling water for 10 seconds, then peel and remove the core and any pieces of hard stem. Cut in half so that all seed chambers are visible and, taking half a tomato at a time in the palm of your hand, squeeze gently until the seeds fall out. Discard the seeds. Chop the tomatoes coarsely. Rinse the herbs, shake dry and chop.

Heat the oil in a frying pan and fry the onions and garlic until they are soft and golden. Add the beans and heat them through. Stir in the tomatoes, and season to taste with salt and pepper. Add the herbs and mix well.

Place the crown roast of lamb on a heated serving plate and remove the string. Arrange the beans in the middle and round the edges of the crown. Serve very hot, with the gravy.

1 **Stretching the joint.** Cut a little way into the meat between every second bone and pull the bones away from one another slightly, bending the meat towards the inside.

2 **Shaping the crown.** Bend the joint round with the fat to the inside until both ends meet. Secure with a wooden toothpick through the upper part of the meat.

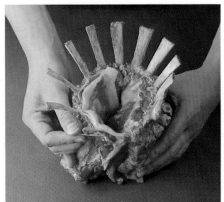

3 **Tying the joint.** Bind the string around the lower part of the joint, pull as tightly as possible and tie with a firm knot. The joint should now be marinated.

4 **Adding the wine and stock.** Mix the wine and stock together, and from time to time add just enough liquid to prevent the herbs and vegetables from burning.

Our tip

When the rib bones are trimmed, the skin and a little meat will be removed; this can be added to a soup or stew so that there is no wastage.

Loin of Lamb with Herbs and Garlic

The spicy crust made of herbs and garlic gives the tender lamb an unusual fragrance. Serve with young French beans and sauté potatoes.

1 whole bulb garlic
1 onion
6 tablespoons veal or beef stock
1 sprig fresh rosemary
2 sprigs fresh thyme
1 bunch fresh parsley
salt
freshly ground black pepper
2 tablespoons Dijon mustard
25 g/1 oz fresh breadcrumbs
4 tablespoons olive oil
1 joint loin of lamb
or best end of neck,
cut right across the
backbone, weighing 1.25 kg/2½ lb

Preparation time: 1½ hours

Bring a saucepan of water to the boil. Peel the cloves of garlic and drop into the boiling water. Bring to the boil again, then drain the garlic and plunge into ice-cold water. Drain again.

Peel the onion and chop coarsely. Place in a small saucepan with the garlic and cover with the stock. Bring to the boil, then simmer over a gentle heat for about 25 minutes or until the onion and garlic are soft.

Meanwhile, rinse the herbs, shake dry and strip the leaves from the stalks. Chop the leaves very finely and place in a bowl.

Put the garlic and onion in an electric blender and reduce to a purée, or chop to a fine pulp. Put in the bowl with the herbs and season to taste with salt and pepper. Mix in the mustard and breadcrumbs. Add a few drops of olive oil and stir until the mixture has a smooth consistency.

Heat the oven to hot (220°C, 425°F, gas 7). Wipe the joint with a damp cloth and pat dry with kitchen paper. Season all over with salt and pepper, and score the fat in a criss-cross pattern with a sharp knife. Heat half the remaining olive oil in a large flameproof casserole or flat roasting tin and brown the meat well on all sides over a high heat.

Spread the garlic and herb mixture evenly over the fat side of the lamb. Smooth it carefully with the back of a spoon. Sprinkle the rest of the oil over the mixture and place the joint on the middle shelf of the heated oven. Cook for 30–40 minutes, or until the meat is cooked to your liking, and the herb crust is golden brown.

Remove the meat from the oven, cover loosely with a sheet of foil and allow to rest in a warm place for 10–15 minutes. Slice the meat lengthways along the backbone and then in slices from the backbone towards the edges. Serve hot.

Our tip

Some people think loin of lamb tastes best when it is a little rare inside. In order to be quite sure when the lamb is ready, use a meat thermometer as in the recipe for leg of lamb (page 00). If you do not have such a thermometer, test the lamb by inserting a metal skewer into the middle of the meat towards the end of the cooking time. If the juices that run out are light pink, the lamb is almost ready; if they are still blood-red, extend the cooking time.

1 **Blanching the garlic.** Place the garlic cloves in the rapidly boiling water and let it return to the boil. Drain the garlic and plunge into ice-cold water. Drain again.

2 **Making the garlic crust.** Mix the garlic and onion purée with the herbs, breadcrumbs, mustard and a few drops of olive oil. Season to taste with salt and pepper and mix to a smooth paste.

3 **Coating the joint.** Spread the herb and garlic mixture on the fat side of the joint and smooth over carefully. Sprinkle over the rest of the oil and place the meat in the oven.

Oriental Lamb Pilaff

Oriental lamb pilaff is a fascinating and unusual mixture of savoury lamb, fresh grapes and sweet sultanas or raisins.

---

450 g/1 lb lean lamb,
from the leg
2 onions
1 clove garlic
1 red pepper
150 g/5 oz seedless grapes
25 g/1 oz sultanas or raisins
65 g/2½ oz butter
salt
freshly ground black pepper
good pinch ground ginger
450 ml/¾ pint hot meat stock
150 g/5 oz patna rice

Preparation time: 45 minutes

Wipe the meat with a damp cloth, pat dry and cut into 2 cm/¾ in cubes. Peel the onions and garlic. Chop the onions finely, and chop or crush the garlic. Halve the red pepper and remove the core and seeds. Rinse in cold water, drain and chop into 2 cm/¾ in squares. Rinse the grapes in warm water, pluck them from the stems and put them to drain in a sieve or colander. Rinse the sultanas or raisins in hot water and place in the sieve with the grapes.

Heat 40 g/1½ oz of the butter in a large frying pan and sear the meat cubes, a few at a time, on all sides over a strong heat. When all the meat has been browned, add the onions and garlic and fry, stirring frequently until they begin to colour. Add the pieces of red pepper and fry them until they are soft. Do not let them brown. Return the meat cubes to the pan.

Place the drained grapes and raisins in the frying pan. Season to taste with salt, pepper and ginger and mix everything together well, being careful not to crush the grapes. Pour the hot stock into the pan, bring to the boil and simmer over a gentle heat for 20–30 minutes.

Meanwhile, place the rice in a sieve and rinse under cold water until the water coming through the rice is clear and therefore free of starch. Drain well. Bring a saucepan of salted water to the boil. Add the rice, stir once and simmer for 10–15 minutes or until tender. It should not be overcooked. Turn the rice back into the sieve and drain thoroughly. Rinse it briefly under cold running water to separate the grains but do not let it get cold.

Dot the rice with the rest of the butter. Mix it in with two forks until it has melted and combined with the rice. Put the rice into a ring mould, press it in lightly and then turn out on to a heated serving dish. Place the lamb mixture in the ring and serve immediately.

1 **Adding the fruit.** Place the drained grapes and raisins or sultanas in the frying pan, season with salt, pepper and ginger and mix everything together without crushing the grapes.

2 **Rinsing the rice.** Rinse the rice under cold running water until the water running out of the sieve is clear and therefore free of starch. Drain well, then cook in salted water.

3 **Mixing in the butter.** Dot the rest of the butter over the rice and mix it in with two forks until it has melted and all the grains of rice are coated. Press into a ring mould.

Our tip

The meat, rice and other ingredients can be cooked together as in a risotto, if preferred. In that case, remove the meat from the pan when it has been well browned and place it in a sieve with a plate underneath to catch any meat juices. Rinse and drain the rice and fry it gently in the frying pan until it becomes glassy in appearance. Add the onion and garlic and proceed as in the recipe. Stir in the meat and any juices at the same time as the fruit and add a double quantity of stock as the rice will require more liquid. Stir occasionally during cooking so that the ingredients cook evenly.

Braised Duck with Red Cabbage

In Germany, braised duck with red cabbage is traditionally served with potato dumplings or plain boiled potatoes. The duck itself is stuffed with apples, chicken livers and herbs and braised in white wine.

100 g/4 oz white bread,
without crusts
250 ml/8 fl oz lukewarm milk
40 g/1½ oz raisins
1 duck, weighing about
1.75 kg/4 lb, with liver
150 g/5 oz chicken livers · 4 apples
75 g/3 oz goose fat or lard ·
salt
freshly ground black pepper
2 sprigs fresh marjoram
small bunch fresh parsley
1 egg · 1 stick celery
1 carrot · 2 onions
250 ml/8 fl oz dry white wine
1 kg/2 lb red cabbage
1 tablespoon sugar
pinch ground allspice
1–2 small bay leaves
2 tablespoons wine vinegar
6 tablespoons water
2 tablespoons redcurrant jelly

Preparation time: 2¼ hours

Place the bread in a bowl, pour the lukewarm milk over it and leave to soak for 15 minutes. Meanwhile, rinse the raisins in hot water and pat dry in a tea towel. Remove any skin, tubes or sinews from the duck liver and chicken livers. Pat dry and chop finely. Peel and core 1½ apples, and chop into small cubes.

Melt 25 g/1 oz of the goose fat or lard in a frying pan and fry the apples and livers over a moderate heat for 5 minutes. Remove from the pan and place in a bowl.

Squeeze the excess milk out of the bread and put the bread in the bowl with the liver and apple mixture. Add the raisins and salt and pepper to taste. Rinse the marjoram and half of the parsley, shake dry and chop very finely. Put the herbs in the bowl, add the egg and mix everything together thoroughly.

Rinse the duck in cold water and pat dry. Season the duck inside and out with salt and pepper, then stuff with the apple and liver mixture. Truss the duck by first pulling the skin round the vent opening together and fastening the edges together with metal skewers or wooden toothpicks. When the skewers or toothpicks are in place, truss the duck by tying the string crossways round the skewers or toothpicks, finishing with a firm knot. Melt 25 g/1 oz of the goose fat or lard in a large saucepan and fry the duck until it is brown on all sides.

Meanwhile, trim the celery. Peel the carrot and one of the onions. Chop the vegetables coarsely. Add them to the pan with the duck and fry until they begin to take on colour. Pour in the wine, cover the pan and simmer gently for about 1½ hours or until the duck is tender.

Once the duck is simmering, prepare the red cabbage. Remove any coarse outer leaves, cut in half and remove the core. Shred finely, rinse and drain. Peel and core the remaining apples. Peel the remaining onion and chop finely. Heat the rest of the goose fat or lard in a saucepan and fry the onion gently until it is soft and golden. Add the shredded cabbage and fry gently, stirring from time to time, until it is almost soft and beginning to fall together. Season with the sugar, allspice, salt, pepper, bay leaves and wine vinegar. Add the water and stir in the apples. Bring to the boil, then cover the pan and simmer over a gentle heat until the cabbage is very tender.

When the duck is ready, take it out of the pan. Remove the trussing string and skewers or toothpicks and keep the duck warm while making the gravy. Skim off as much fat as possible from the stock, then strain it and return to the pan. Boil

rapidly over a high heat to reduce. Once again, skim off as much fat as possible and season to taste with salt and pepper.

Stir the redcurrant jelly into the red cabbage. Discard the bay leaves and place the cabbage on a large heated serving plate. Place the duck whole or carved on the bed of red cabbage. Garnish with the rest of the parsley and serve hot, with the gravy.

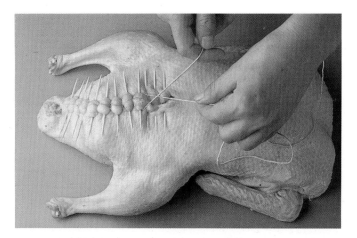

1 **Trussing the duck.** Pull the skin together round the vent and fasten the edges with metal skewers or wooden toothpicks. Tie the string round the skewers or toothpicks and across the vent.

2 **Cooking the red cabbage.** Stir in the pieces of apple and add the water at the same time. Bring to the boil, then cover and reduce the heat. Simmer until the cabbage is tender.

3 **Preparing the gravy.** Skim as much fat as possible from the stock, strain it and then boil down over a high heat. Skim off the fat again, and season with salt and pepper.

Chicken Breast with Figs

Chicken breast with figs, deep-fried in small greaseproof paper packets, can be served on many occasions – as a starter or hors d'oeuvre or as an appetizer or snack during an informal party. They can also be served as a light main course accompanied by green salad and potato straws or rice.

4 chicken breasts, each weighing 100 g/4 oz, without skin and bones
6–8 dried figs
2 tablespoons white port or dry sherry
5–6 tablespoons soy sauce
1 orange
cayenne pepper
freshly ground black pepper
salt
2 tablespoons cornflour
oil for deep frying

To marinate: 2 hours
Preparation time: 45 minutes

Wipe the chicken breasts with a damp cloth, pat dry and cut into pieces about 4–5 cm/1¾–2 in in size. Rinse the figs under hot water, dry thoroughly and cut into slices.

To make the marinade, pour the port or sherry into a bowl and stir in 2 tablespoons of the soy sauce. Rinse the orange in hot water, dry thoroughly and grate about half the rind (not the white pith) into the bowl. Halve the orange and squeeze the juice from one half. Stir it into the port mixture and season to taste with cayenne pepper and pepper but only a little salt since there is salt in the soy sauce. Place the chicken and figs in the bowl and turn them a few times in the marinade. Cover the bowl and leave them to marinate for 1½ hours.

Remove the figs from the marinade and set aside. In order to give the chicken a particularly tender crust when frying, take a little of the marinade from the bowl and mix it with the cornflour, then stir this carefully into the marinade in the bowl. Cover the bowl again and leave the chicken pieces to marinate in this mixture for a further 30 minutes.

Prepare the paper cases by cutting out 14-cm/5½-in squares from greaseproof paper. Smooth them out on the work surface. Heat the oil to about 180°C/350°F in a deep frying pan. If you do not have a deep frying thermometer, test the temperature of the oil by frying a cube of bread in it. If the cube turns brown in 10 seconds, then the oil has reached the correct temperature.

Drain the chicken pieces and pat them dry. Place one piece in the middle of every paper square and place a slice of fig on top. Brush the corners of the paper with the remaining soy sauce. Close the packets by folding over two opposite corners and pressing them firmly together. Now fold over the remaining corners and hold them firmly in your fingers until the paper sticks together.

Place a few packets at a time in the hot oil and fry for 5–7 minutes or until they are golden brown. Remove from the oil with a slotted spoon and place on a thick layer of kitchen paper to drain. Place on heated plates and serve immediately. Let your guests open the packets at the table so that none of the aroma is lost.

1 **Marinating the chicken and figs.** Place the chicken and figs in the marinade and turn to coat on all sides. Cover the bowl and leave for 1½ hours before removing the figs.

2 **Preparing the paper packets.** Remove the chicken from the marinade, pat dry and place one piece in the middle of every paper square. Top with a slice of fig.

3 **Sealing the packets.** Brush the corners of the paper with soy sauce. Fold two opposite corners together and press firmly together. Fold over the remaining corners and press until they stick.

Coq au Vin de Bourgogne

There are many recipes for coq au vin – chicken cooked in wine – but coq au vin Burgundy style is one of the most delicious.

---

1 plump roasting chicken,
weighing 1.25 kg/2¾ lb
salt
freshly ground white pepper
225 g/8 oz young carrots
225 g/8 oz spring onions
225 g/8 oz small button
mushrooms
1 stick celery
1 carrot
65 g/2½ oz streaky bacon
in a piece
2 tablespoons oil
40 g/1½ oz butter
3 cloves garlic
1 tablespoon flour
450 ml/¾ pint red
Burgundy wine
2 sprigs fresh thyme
1 sprig fresh tarragon
small bunch fresh parsley
1 bay leaf
water or chicken stock
100 g/4 oz chicken livers
2 tablespoons brandy
2 slices white bread

Preparation time: 2 hours

Rinse the chicken inside and out under cold running water and dry thoroughly. Divide into serving-sized pieces. This is done as follows: remove the legs and thighs by bending them as far as possible from the body and separating them directly at the joint with a sharp knife or poultry shears. Separate the thigh from the drumstick by straightening the leg slightly and dividing it at the joint. Cut the wings off at the joint. Cut the body in half along the breastbone, then cut the two halves into two or three pieces crossways. Dry the chicken pieces again and season with salt and pepper. Rub the seasoning in with the palm of your hand.

Heat the oven to moderate (180°C, 350°F, gas 4). Scrape the young carrots. Trim the spring onions, and put the green stalks on one side. Clean the mushrooms.

Trim and finely chop the celery. Peel and dice the carrot. Remove any rind from the bacon and cut the bacon into 1-cm/½-in cubes. Blanch them in boiling water for 2 minutes, then drain.

Heat the oil and 15 g/½ oz of the butter in a large flameproof casserole. Fry the bacon until it is golden brown, then remove from the pot. Brown the white part of the spring onions and the young carrots in the fat for 5 minutes, stirring frequently. Add the mushrooms and fry for a further 5 minutes. Remove the vegetables with a slotted spoon. Fry the chicken pieces, a few at a time, until they are golden on all sides.

Peel and chop the garlic and mix it with the chopped celery and carrot. Place these vegetables in the pot and fry until golden brown. Return the chicken pieces to the pot and sprinkle the flour over the chicken and vegetables. Continue to fry until the flour is well browned. Pour the red wine into the casserole, stir well and add the bacon, spring onions, mushrooms and young carrots.

Rinse the thyme, tarragon and parsley and shake dry. Tie the herbs into a bunch together with the bay leaf. Place in the casserole and top up the liquid with water or stock so that everything is just half covered. Cover the casserole and place in the heated oven. Cook for 45 minutes.

Shortly before the end of cooking time, prepare the chicken livers. Pat them dry and chop very finely. Melt 15 g/½ oz of the butter in a frying pan and fry the livers for 30 seconds to 1 minute over a gentle heat. Press them through a sieve or blend in a liquidiser and mix with the brandy.

Remove the crusts from the bread and halve the slices diagonally. Melt the rest of the butter in the frying pan and fry the bread until golden on both sides. Drain on kitchen paper.

Remove the chicken and vegetables from the casserole and keep warm. Discard the bunch of herbs and boil down the liquid on top of the stove until it is well reduced. Remove the pot from the heat and stir in the liver and brandy mixture. Taste and adjust the seasoning. Put the chicken and vegetables back into the casserole and heat everything through again. Do not boil.

Rinse the green spring onion stalks and chop them into thin rings. Serve the coq au vin garnished with the green onion rings and triangles of fried bread.

1 **Removing the chicken legs.** Pull the leg as far as possible from the body and cut through the joint with a sharp knife or poultry shears. Repeat with the other leg.

2 **Jointing the legs.** Straighten the leg and cut the thigh from the drumstick at the joint. Then remove the wings and cut the body in half lengthways.

3 **Frying the vegetables.** Brown the white part of the spring onions and young carrots in hot fat for 5 minutes, then add the mushrooms and continue frying.

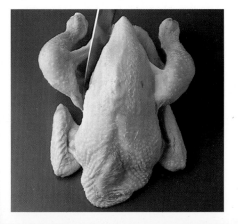

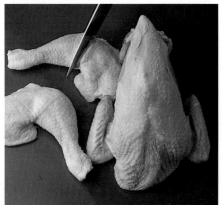

4 **Adding the flour.** As soon as the diced vegetables have taken on colour, sprinkle the flour over and let it brown. Add the red wine, vegetables and bacon.

Our tip

If you like garlic, rub the slices of bread with a little crushed garlic before frying them in butter or add a few chopped cloves of garlic to the frying pan. Real garlic enthusiasts sprinkle finely chopped garlic on the bread after frying it.

Rabbit Stew

Mushrooms, vegetables and herbs give this spicy rabbit stew its wonderful flavour. It is easy to make and relatively low in calories.

1 rabbit, weighing
1–1.25 kg/2–2½ lb
2 tablespoons made mustard
2 tablespoons brandy
1 leek
2 onions
225 g/8 oz carrots
450 g/1 lb mixed mushrooms
(chanterelles, yellow boletus
and button mushrooms, for example)
1–2 cloves garlic
small bunch fresh parsley
2 sprigs fresh thyme
1–2 leaves celery
3 tablespoons olive oil
15 g/½ oz butter
150 ml/¼ pint dry white wine
150 ml/¼ pint hot chicken
or beef stock
salt
freshly ground black pepper
2 large ripe tomatoes
1 small bay leaf
2 dried juniper berries
1 clove
4 tablespoons double cream

To marinate: 30 minutes
Preparation time: 1¼ hours

Ask your butcher to skin and divide the rabbit into eight neat joints. Wipe the joints with a damp cloth and pat them dry. Stir the mustard and brandy together to make a smooth paste and brush the joints all over with it. Cover and leave to marinate for 30 minutes.

Trim the leek and cut on a slant into pieces 2 cm/¾ in wide. Put in a sieve and rinse to remove any grit that might remain. Put aside to drain.

Peel the onions and slice into thin rings. Peel the carrots. Cut into quarters lengthways, then cut across into pieces 2 cm/¾ in wide. Clean the mushrooms and chop coarsely. Peel and finely chop the garlic. Rinse the parsley, thyme and celery leaves and shake dry. Chop very finely.

Heat the oil and butter in a large flameproof casserole and fry the pieces of rabbit for 5–10 minutes over a high heat until they begin to brown. Add the vegetables to the casserole and fry, stirring frequently, until lightly browned. Add the herbs and garlic. Pour in about half the wine and bring to the boil, stirring all the time to loosen any meat sediments in the pan. Then add the rest of the wine and the stock and return to the boil. Boil for 1–2 minutes, then season to taste with salt and pepper.

Scald the tomatoes in boiling water for 10 seconds, then peel and remove the core and any pieces of hard stem. Halve the tomatoes so that all seed chambers are visible and, taking half a tomato at a time in the palm of your hand, squeeze gently until the seeds fall out. Discard the seeds. Chop the tomatoes coarsely. Put them in the casserole together with the bay leaf, juniper berries, the clove and any remaining mustard and brandy marinade. Reduce the heat, cover tightly and simmer over a gentle heat for 30–40 minutes.

Stir in the cream and simmer until the gravy has thickened a little. Season to taste with salt and pepper, discard the bay leaf, juniper berries and clove, and serve. Boiled noodles tossed in butter, boiled potatoes or fresh white bread go well with this dish.

1 **Preparing the leek.** Trim off the root end and dark green leaves, then cut on a slant into pieces 2 cm/¾ in wide. Place in a sieve and rinse in cold water to remove any grit.

2 **Browning the vegetables.** Place the prepared vegetables in the casserole and brown them a little on all sides, stirring frequently. Add the garlic and herbs.

3 **Loosening the meat sediments.** Pour in about half the wine and bring to the boil, stirring all the time to loosen any meat sediments in the casserole. Add the rest of the wine and the stock.

Our tip

Rabbit is usually stewed because it is very lean and inclined to become dry if cooked in any other way. When you are browning the rabbit, make sure that it develops a thin crust which will protect the meat inside. Do not season the meat with salt before searing it as salt draws the juices out of meat. When stewing the rabbit, make sure that the casserole lid is tightly closed and that the stew does not boil. When the stew is ready the meat should be so tender that it practically falls from the bones.

Vol-au-Vent with Ragout of Venison

It is not really as difficult as it looks to make a vol-au-vent case, but peace and quiet and plenty of time are essential for success. It is also important to rest the case in a cool place before baking it. This allows the pastry to lose tension and ensures even rising.

Serves 8

---

3 packets (350 g/12 oz each)
frozen puff pastry
2 egg yolks
450 g/1 lb venison chops or steak
150 g/5 oz chanterelles or
other mushrooms
150 g/5 oz button mushrooms
juice $\frac{1}{2}$ lemon · 2 onions
2 tender young carrots
2 cloves garlic · 25 g/1 oz butter
1 tablespoon oil · salt
freshly ground black pepper
1 tablespoon plain flour
6 tablespoons full-bodied dry red wine
6 tablespoons hot meat stock
2 sprigs fresh thyme
1 sprig fresh rosemary
1 juniper berry
1–2 teaspoons German mustard
150 g/5 oz frozen broccoli
6 tablespoons double cream
1 tablespoon rose hip syrup
small bunch fresh parsley

To thaw: about 30 minutes
Preparation time: $1\frac{1}{2}$–2 hours

Spread out the sheets of pastry on a work surface and leave to thaw. Meanwhile, make the foil hemisphere which will be used to shape the vol-au-vent case. Line a round-bottomed bowl with aluminium foil. The edges of the foil should stand up above the rim of the bowl to a height of 10 cm/4 in. Pack the lined bowl with small pieces of greaseproof paper, then fold the edges of the foil over the top to form a hemisphere.

Brush half the sheets of pastry with cold water and place them on top of one another. Roll out the dough on a floured surface to 3 mm/$\frac{1}{8}$ in thick. Place the foil hemisphere, flat side down, in the centre of the pastry. Cut around the foil shape leaving a margin 6 cm/$2\frac{1}{2}$ in wide. Then cut another circle 6 cm/$2\frac{1}{2}$ in away from the first circle. First remove the excess pastry, then carefully remove the

6 cm/$2\frac{1}{2}$ in wide pastry ring and put it aside for use later.

Roll out the remaining sheets of pastry in the same manner as before and lay the pastry over the foil hemisphere. Trim the edges and press lightly onto the pastry base. If necessary, brush the edges with water before pressing them together.

For the vol-au-vent lid, cut out three or four pastry rings which diminish in size, in other words one large, one medium and two small. Cut shapes from the excess pastry to decorate the sides of the pastry case.

Brush the entire surface of the case with beaten egg yolk. Lay the rounds for the lid on top of one another, brushing each pastry round with egg yolk, and place them on top of the pastry case. Arrange the pastry decorations on the sides. Brush the margin of pastry round the foil hemisphere with beaten egg yolk and place the pastry ring on top. Press it on lightly and brush with egg yolk. Leave to rest in a cool place for 15 minutes. Meanwhile, heat the oven to hot (220°c, 425°F, gas 7).

Carefully transfer the pastry case to a dampened baking sheet. Place in the heated oven and bake for 20–25 minutes or until golden brown.

Meanwhile, prepare the ragout. Remove any bones from the meat, then cut the meat into 1 cm/$\frac{1}{2}$ in cubes. Clean and chop the mushrooms and sprinkle the button mushrooms with lemon juice to prevent discoloration. Peel the onions, carrots and garlic and chop them finely.

Heat the butter and oil in a large frying pan. Brown the meat cubes well on all sides and remove from the pan. Fry the mushrooms in small portions, then remove from the pan and season to taste with salt and pepper. Fry the rest of the vegetables until golden brown, then sprinkle the flour over them. Fry, stirring, until the flour is browned. Pour in the wine and stock. Rinse, shake dry and chop the thyme and rosemary. Crush the juniper berry. Place the herbs and juniper berry in the pan and season with the mustard. Return the meat cubes. Bring to the boil and simmer for 20 minutes.

Meanwhile, cook the broccoli in boiling salted water for 3 minutes. Drain well and chop the broccoli into smaller pieces. Add to the pan with the cream and rose hip syrup. Stir well, then return the mushrooms. Boil down the liquid until it is creamy. Rinse, shake dry and chop the

parsley. Stir into the ragoût and keep warm.

Remove the pastry case from the oven. Use the largest pastry cutter (with which the largest pastry round for the lid was made) and a pointed knife to remove the lid. The paper must now be removed from the pastry case. This is done by leaving the pastry cutter in the pastry to act as a chimney and pulling out the pieces of paper and foil carefully through it. In this way the pastry will not be damaged.

Season the ragoût with salt and pepper to taste and pour it into the pastry case through the pastry cutter chimney. Remove the cutter, put on the lid and serve the vol-au-vent.

Our tip

This vol-au-vent case can also be used for many other fillings, for example chicken or veal fricassée with vegetables, fish ragoût or mussels or snails in cream sauce. If you do not have time to bake the pastry case yourself, buy small vol-au-vent cases from your baker and serve this venison ragoût in them.

1 **Cutting out the circles.** Cut two circles around the foil hemisphere with 6cm/2½in distance between them, and 6cm/2½in between the first circle and the foil shape. Put the excess pastry and the pastry ring aside for later use.

2 **Shaping the vol-au-vent case.** Roll out the remaining pastry, lay it over the hemisphere and trim the edges. Press lightly on to the pastry base, first moistening if necessary.

3 **Putting the pastry ring in place.** Brush the margin with beaten egg yolk and lay the pastry ring on top. Press it on lightly and brush with more egg yolk.

4 **Removing the paper.** Remove the lid with the pastry cutter and a sharp knife. Leave the pastry cutter in place and pull the paper and foil out of the case.

Stuffed Pheasant with Cider Sauce

Apples are often used to give a fresh fruity sauce to game. In this recipe the apple flavour is intensified by the addition of calvados and dry cider.

½ stale bread roll
100 g/4 oz chicken livers
25 g/1 oz streaky bacon
1½ onions · 5 Granny Smith apples
¼ lemon · salt
freshly ground black pepper
small bunch fresh parsley
2 sprigs fresh lemon
balm (optional)
1 egg yolk
1 pheasant, weighing
800 g/1¾ lb, dressed
4–8 slices pork fat or
rashers streaky bacon
40 g/1½ oz butter
1 tablespoon oil
250 ml/8 fl oz dry cider
1 tablespoon calvados
2 tablespoons double cream

Preparation time: 1¼ hours

To make the stuffing, cut the roll into slices and soak in lukewarm water for 5 minutes. Meanwhile, clean the chicken livers. Remove any rind from the bacon and chop the bacon. Peel the half onion and one of the apples. Cut both into quarters and core the apple. Mince the livers, bacon, onion and apple finely or process in a food processor. Place in a bowl.

Squeeze the excess water from the bread. Tear the bread into pieces and place in the bowl. Rinse the lemon with hot water, pat dry and grate the rind into the bowl. Season to taste with salt and pepper. Rinse the parsley, shake it dry and chop finely. Place in the bowl. Add the egg yolk and mix everything together well.

Heat the oven to hot (220°C, 425°F, gas 7). Rinse the pheasant inside and out under cold running water. Dry thoroughly and season lightly inside with salt and pepper. Stuff the pheasant and sew up the vent. To truss the pheasant, lay a long piece of string under the tail, cross the string over the front of the tail and bind an end round each leg. Pull the ends tightly and turn the pheasant over without letting go of the string. Run the string alone one side of the bird, over the thigh

and wing, right across the wattle (neck) to bind the other wing before securing with a firm knot. Bard the pheasant on all sides with the pork fat or bacon rashers and truss it again to keep the fat in place.

Peel the remaining onion and two of the apples. Core the apples, then chop the apples and onion.

Heat a roasting tin on top of the stove. Place the pheasant in the tin, breast down. The fat from the barding should soon start to run. Fry, turning, until the barding fat is crisp, then add 15 g/½ oz of the butter and the oil to the tin and place the chopped apples and onion around the pheasant. Fry, stirring, until they begin to take on colour. Turn the pheasant breast up. Add the cider and calvados and bring to the boil, stirring to loosen any sedi-

ments in the tin. Cover the tin and place in the heated oven. Roast for 35 minutes, basting the pheasant frequently with the juices in the tin.

Take the tin from the oven and remove the trussing strings and barding fat from the pheasant. Spread 15 g/½ oz of the butter over the breast. Place in the oven again, without the lid, and let the pheasant brown for a further 10 minutes. Remove from the tin, cover with foil and keep warm.

Strain the stock through a fine sieve into a saucepan and skim off any fat. Stir in the cream and boil to reduce the sauce until it is creamy in consistency. Taste and adjust the seasoning, and keep warm.

Peel and core the remaining apples and cut across into rings. Heat the remaining

butter in a frying pan and fry the rings until they are golden on both sides. Place on kitchen paper to drain.

Serve the pheasant, garnished with the apple rings and remaining lemon balm, if used. Serve the sauce separately.

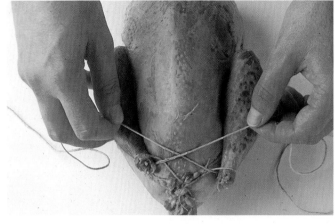

1 **Trussing the pheasant.** Lay a long piece of string under the tail, cross it over at the front and bind an end round each leg. Pull the string tightly and turn the pheasant over.

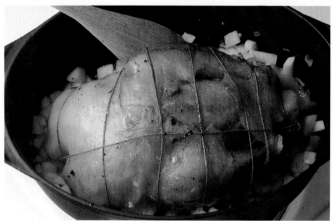

2 **Frying the apples and onions.** Melt 15 g/½ oz of the butter and the oil in the roasting tin, add the chopped apples and onions and fry gently until they are golden brown.

3 **Frying the apple rings.** Melt the rest of the butter in a frying pan and fry the apple rings until they are golden on both sides. Drain off the fat on kitchen paper.

Chicken Baked in Clay

Chicken baked in clay belongs to the category of culinary surprises – it will certainly amuse and entertain your guests. More important is the fact that it is one of the most delectable of dishes since the clay completely seals the flavour in.

---

10 bunches assorted fresh herbs
2–4 cloves garlic
½ lemon
1 plump roasting chicken,
weighing about 1.25 kg/2¾ lb
salt
freshly ground white pepper
25 g/1 oz butter, softened
about 4 kg/9 lb fresh
damp clay (obtainable at
arts and crafts shops)

Preparation time: at least 2 hours

Before preparing the chicken, light the charcoal grill in which the chicken is to be baked. The charcoal must be at least 10 cm/4 in high in the grate or grill. Make a good fire and leave to burn until covered with grey ash and glowing red when blown on.

Rinse the bunches of herbs, shake them thoroughly dry and mix them well. If they are not well mixed, the chicken may well taste strongly of thyme on one side and lovage on the other. Peel the cloves of garlic, slice them thinly and mix them with the herbs. Rinse the lemon under hot water, dry thoroughly and grate off the rind.

Rinse the chicken inside and out under cold running water. Dry thoroughly. Rub the chicken inside and out with salt, pepper and the grated lemon rind. Spread the butter over the chicken or chop it into small pieces and place inside the chicken.

Cover the work surface with a large sheet of thick plastic or a plastic bin bag which has been cut open. (It would be difficult to lift the heavy clay from the surface without the plastic.) Place the clay in the middle of the plastic sheet. Wet your hands and push the clay from the centre towards the edges of the plastic sheet until you have a large flat round of clay about 2.5 cm/1 in thick. It should be large enough to wrap round the chicken. Wet your hands again and smooth over the surface of the clay until there are no cracks to be seen and the surface is quite smooth.

Lay one-third of the herbs in the centre of the clay round and place the chicken on top. Arrange the rest of the herbs over the chicken so that it is completely covered. Use the foil to lift the clay from the work surface and wrap it over the chicken. Press the edges of the clay together with wet hands and rub over the joins until they are quite smooth. During this process try to avoid stretching or pulling the clay as this might result in cracks or some parts of the clay shell being thinner than the rest. It is important that the clay is equally thick all over to ensure even cooking.

Place the clay parcel in the glowing fire and heap up some of the hot charcoal

round the edges. The chicken will take 1½ hours to bake.

When it is ready, remove the clay parcel from the fire with flameproof gloves. Place it on a thick board and use a hammer to crack it open; it will be as hard as stone. Remove the pieces of clay carefully so that they do not crumble over the chicken. If any small pieces of clay do fall on the chicken, brush them off with a pastry brush. Remove the herbs from the chicken and serve immediately.

1 **Covering the chicken with herbs.** Place one-third of the herbs in the centre of the clay round and lay the chicken on top of them. Cover with the rest of the herbs.

2 **Wrapping up the chicken.** Lift the clay from the work surface with the help of the plastic foil. Wrap it carefully round the chicken and seal it with wet hands.

3 **Baking the chicken.** Place the clay parcel on the thick bed of glowing charcoal. Heap up some of the charcoal around the edges and bake for 1½ hours.

4 **Opening the clay parcel.** Remove the clay from the fire with flameproof gloves, place it on a board and crack it open with a hammer. Remove the clay carefully.

Sweet and Sour Chicken

Sweet and sour chicken must be served very quickly or the vegetables and the crisp batter round the chicken may become soft. Boiled rice and warm sake (rice wine) are the traditional accompaniments.

575 g/1¼ lb chicken breasts, without skin and bone
1 egg
25 g/1 oz plain flour
25 g/1 oz cornflour
salt
freshly ground white pepper
2 tablespoons soy sauce
2 tablespoons rice wine or dry sherry
250 ml/8 fl oz cold chicken stock
1 green pepper
2 carrots
1 leek
1 onion
150 g/5 oz Chinese cabbage
4 slices canned pineapple
1–2 cloves garlic
peanut or vegetable oil for deep frying
2 tablespoons peanut oil
1½ tablespoons sugar
2–3 tablespoons red wine vinegar
1–2 tablespoons tomato ketchup

Preparation time: 1 hour

Pat the chicken breasts dry with kitchen paper and cut them into pieces about 2.5 cm/1 in in size.

Separate the egg, and set the white aside. Place the egg yolk, flour and cornflour in a bowl and season with salt and pepper. Add 1 tablespoon of the soy sauce and rice wine or sherry and a little of the chicken stock and mix to a smooth batter. It should not be too thin. Leave for 30 minutes.

Meanwhile, prepare the vegetables. Halve the green pepper, remove the seeds and core and cut into pieces 2 cm/¾ in in size. Peel the carrots and score notches in them lengthways. Cut them into slices; these will be flower-shaped. Trim the leek, halve lengthways and rinse thoroughly under cold running water. Drain and cut into 2-cm/¾-in lengths. Peel the onion and cut into quarters. Pull the layers of onion apart. Rinse the cabbage, drain and cut into pieces 2 cm/¾ in in size. Drain the pineapple slices and chop into 2-cm/¾-in pieces as well. Peel the garlic and chop finely or crush.

Heat the oil in a deep frying pan to 180°C/350°F. Heat the oven to very cool (120°C, 250°F, gas ½). Place a baking sheet in the oven to heat at the same time.

Beat the egg white to stiff peaks, then fold it loosely into the batter. Place the chicken pieces in the batter, a few at a time. Turn the chicken pieces in the batter, then deep fry in portions until golden brown. Drain on kitchen paper and place on the baking sheets in the heated oven to keep warm while the remaining chicken is fried.

Heat 2 tablespoons of peanut oil in a frying pan and stir-fry the carrots, green peppers, leek, onion, cabbage and garlic over a high heat for about 5 minutes. The vegetables should become golden but not brown. Sprinkle the sugar over the vegetables and as soon as it has melted and become golden brown, add the wine vinegar, the rest of the chicken stock and the tomato ketchup. Stir in the pineapple pieces and cook over a high heat for 1–2 minutes. Season to taste with salt and pepper and add the remaining soy sauce and rice wine or sherry. Add the fried chicken pieces and mix in quickly. Serve immediately before the vegetables or chicken can go soft.

1 **Slicing the carrots.** Peel the carrots and score them lengthways with three or four notches before cutting them into slices which will be flower-shaped.

2 **Frying the chicken.** Coat the chicken pieces in the batter and fry in portions until the pieces are golden brown. Drain on kitchen paper and keep warm.

3 **Adding the stock.** As soon as the sugar melts and becomes golden brown, add the wine vinegar, the rest of the stock and the ketchup. Stir in the pineapple pieces.

4 **Stirring in the chicken.** Stir the fried chicken pieces quickly into the vegetables. Serve immediately, so there is no time for the batter on the chicken to soften.

Our tip

The preparation is of utmost importance in this recipe as all the ingredients should retain a certain crispness. Fry the chicken in small portions so that the batter becomes crisp and place the pieces next to one another on the baking sheet in the oven and not on top of one another, otherwise the crisp batter will become soft. Mix the chicken with the vegetables quickly and serve immediately.

Hazelnut Pudding with Chocolate Sauce

Old-fashioned desserts are often the ones that everybody loves best. This hazelnut pudding is an excellent example of a steamed pudding – juicy, light and delicately fluffy, and with a melting sweetness which is irresistible.

Serves 8

100 g/4 oz shelled hazelnuts
25 g/1 oz macaroons
1 vanilla pod
65 g/2½ oz caster sugar
2 eggs
1 tablespoon amaretto
(almond liqueur)
pinch salt
40 g/1½ oz plain flour
pinch baking powder
25 g/1 oz butter
butter for greasing basin
1 tablespoon fine fresh
breadcrumbs
100 g/4 oz plain chocolate
150 ml/¼ pint double cream

Preparation time: 1¼ hours

Heat the oven to hot (220°c, 425°F, gas 7). Spread out the hazelnuts on a baking sheet and toast them in the heated oven until the skins begin to split. This will take 8–10 minutes, depending on the age of the nuts. Remove from the oven and pour the nuts from the sheet on to a tea towel. Rub them in the towel until the skins fall off, then spread them out and leave to cool.

Put the macaroons in a polythene bag and crush them finely with a rolling pin. Alternatively, use a food processor. Place the vanilla pod on the work surface and, holding it firmly, slit it open lengthways. Scrape out the vanilla seeds and pulp with the tip of a sharp knife. Mix 40 g/1½ oz of the caster sugar with the seeds and pulp. When the hazelnuts have cooled, grind them in a nut mill or food processor. Put aside 1 tablespoon of the ground nuts for use later.

Separate the eggs into two bowls: the whites into a large one and the yolks into a smaller heatproof one. Place the small bowl over a pan of simmering water. Beat the egg yolks and amaretto together with a rotary whisk or electric beater until frothy. Gradually add the vanilla and sugar mixture and continue beating until the mixture is pale and creamy. Remove from the heat. Beat the egg whites with the salt until stiff peaks form. Gradually add the remaining sugar, beating constantly. Spoon the egg white mixture on to the egg yolk mixture. Sift the flour and baking powder over the egg white mixture in the bowl. Add the ground hazelnuts and crushed macaroons and fold

everything gently but thoroughly together with a metal spoon.

Melt the butter over a gentle heat; do not let it brown. Remove from the heat and cool to lukewarm, then pour it into the hazelnut mixture in a thin stream. Fold it in lightly.

Grease a 1 litre/1¾ pint pudding basin or mould thickly with butter. Mix the breadcrumbs with the reserved tablespoon of ground hazelnuts and sprinkle them over the sides of the basin. Pour the hazelnut mixture into the basin – it should not be more than three-quarters full. Cover tightly with a lid, or greased greaseproof paper and foil tied on securely with string.

Place the basin in a steamer or deep, narrow-sided saucepan and pour enough boiling water into the pan to come three-quarters of the way up the sides of the basin. Cover and simmer gently for 1 hour, adding more water when necessary. Do not let the water boil.

Shortly before the end of cooking time, break the chocolate into pieces and place in a heavy saucepan (or the top of a double saucepan) with the cream. Stir constantly over a gentle heat until the chocolate has melted and blended with the cream.

Remove the lid from the pudding basin and wait for a few seconds for the steam to rise from the pudding before turning it out on to a serving plate. Pour the chocolate sauce over the pudding and serve immediately. If any of the pudding is left over, it can be served cold as cake.

1 **Skinning the hazelnuts.** Toast the nuts in a heated oven, then rub off the brown skins in a tea towel. Spread out the nuts and leave to cool before grinding.

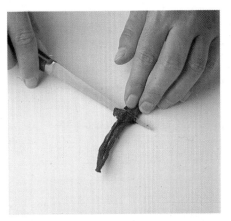
2 **Removing the vanilla pulp.** Slit open the vanilla pod lengthways and scrape out the seeds and pulp with the point of a knife. Mix the seeds and pulp with sugar.

3 **Folding in the butter.** Pour the cooled melted butter into the hazelnut mixture in a thin stream. Fold in gently, then pour into the prepared basin.

Honey Parfait with Strawberry Sauce

Parfaits are amongst the finest and creamiest iced desserts. Try this unusual combination of sweet honey parfait with a delicately tart strawberry sauce.

---

1 egg
1 egg yolk
25 g/1 oz caster sugar
50 g/2 oz acacia or
clover honey
250 ml/8 fl oz double cream
1–2 tablespoons framboise
(raspberry eau-de-vie) or kirsch

For the strawberry sauce:
225 g/8 oz unsweetened
strawberry purée, sieved
1–1½ tablespoons caster
sugar or to taste
juice ½ lemon
2 tablespoons framboise
(raspberry eau-de-vie) or kirsch

Preparation time: 30 minutes
To chill: 2–2¼ hours

Place the egg and the egg yolk in a heatproof bowl and beat them with an electric beater until they are pale and frothy. Gradually add the sugar, beating all the time. Place the bowl over a pan of simmering (not boiling) water and continue to beat. When the mixture has the consistency of thick cream, beat in the honey.

Remove the bowl from the hot water and place it in a large bowl of cold water. Continue beating until the mixture has cooled, but is very light and frothy. Do not stop beating until you have reached this stage.

Pour the cream into another bowl and whip until it is thick. Spoon the cream on to the surface of the egg mixture and fold it in very gently. Do not stir. Fold in the eau-de-vie or kirsch. Pour the parfait mixture into four freezerproof moulds, each with a capacity of 150 ml/¼ pint. Smooth over the surface of the mixture, cover and place in the freezer. Freeze for 2–2½ hours. After this time the parfaits should be firm but not hard.

To make the sauce, mix the strawberry purée with the sugar and lemon juice. Cover and put aside for the sugar to dissolve and pervade the mixture. Add the eau-de-vie just before serving.

Dip the moulds in hot water for a few seconds, then turn out the parfaits on to individual plates. Pour a little sauce over each one and serve immediately.

1 **Adding the honey.** Pour the honey into the egg mixture, beating all the time. Remove the bowl from the hot water and place in a large bowl of cold water.

2 **Folding in the cream.** Fold the whipped cream into the mixture gently. Do not stir. Add the eau-de-vie or kirsch at the final stage of folding.

3 **Filling the moulds.** Pour the mixture into four freezerproof moulds, each with a capacity of 150 ml/¼ pint. Smooth over the surface and freeze for 2–2½ hours.

4 **Turning out the parfaits.** Dip the moulds in hot water for a few seconds then turn them out on to individual plates. Pour a little sauce over each one and serve.

Our tip

Restaurants use small metal moulds for parfaits because they quickly become very cold. If you do not have appropriate moulds, use plastic yoghurt tubs or freezerproof cups. If you make the parfait the day before you intend to serve it, remove the moulds from the freezer an hour before serving and place in the refrigerator to thaw slightly.

Clafoutis aux Cerises

A clafoutis is something between a dessert and a fruity cake and can therefore be served with afternoon tea as well.

800 g/1¾ lb dark sweet
cherries, fresh or frozen
40 g/1½ oz plain flour
pinch salt
25 g/1 oz vanilla sugar
75 g/3 oz caster sugar
3 eggs
6 tablespoons milk
2 tablespoons kirsch
butter for greasing dish
fine fresh breadcrumbs for lining dish
65–75 g/2½-3 oz icing sugar

Preparation time: 45 minutes

Rinse the fresh cherries and drain them on a thick layer of kitchen paper or pat them dry in a tea towel. Thaw frozen cherries. Remove the stalks and stones. Heat the oven to moderately hot (200°c, 400°F, gas 6).

Sift the flour into a bowl. Add the salt and the vanilla and caster sugars. Mix everything well together.

Break the eggs into another bowl and beat them with a fork until the yolks have completely combined with the whites. Beat the milk into the mixture. Pour the egg and milk mixture gradually into the flour mixture, whisking all the time until the mixture is quite smooth. Add the kirsch. Pass the cake mixture through a sieve into another bowl to remove any lumps of flour or egg white.

Generously butter a 20-cm/8-in diameter soufflé or other ovenproof dish. Sprinkle the breadcrumbs over the bottom and sides of the dish. Place the cherries in the dish, then pour the cake mixture evenly over them. The cherries should be almost covered. Sprinkle the top so thickly with sifted icing sugar that the cherries can hardly be seen.

Place on the middle shelf of the heated oven and bake for 25–30 minutes until set. Remove from the oven and sprinkle generously with sifted icing sugar once more. Serve hot or cold.

1 **Straining the mixture.** Whisk the cake mixture until quite smooth, then strain through a sieve into another bowl to remove any lumps of flour or egg white.

2 **Filling the dish.** Place the cherries in the prepared ovenproof dish and pour the cake mixture over them as evenly as possible. The cherries should be almost covered.

3 **Covering with icing sugar.** Sift the icing sugar thickly over the pudding so that the cherries can hardly be seen. Place in the heated oven and bake until set.

Our tip

In France clafoutis is generally made from fresh dark juicy cherries – never with canned or bottled fruit. However, if cherries are not in season, the recipe can be made with golden mirabelles, Victoria plums, small dark plums or greengages. The quality of the fruit is decisive for the fresh flavour of the dessert. In order to intensify the fruit flavour you might like to add a little of the appropriate fruit eau-de vie.

Crème Caramel

Crème caramel is a delicious combination of creamy vanilla custard and caramel sauce. It is surprising that this dessert has the reputation of being difficult to make. It is not difficult, but it is important to prepare everything beforehand so that the various stages can follow one another in the right order fairly quickly.

16 sugar lumps
7 tablespoons water
250 ml/8 fl oz milk
6 tablespoons double cream
1 vanilla pod
2 eggs
2 egg yolks
pinch salt
65 g/2½ oz sugar
butter for greasing moulds

Preparation time: 1½ hours
To chill: at least 4 hours

First prepare the lids for six individual moulds of about 120 ml/4 fl oz capacity. Cut out rounds of greaseproof paper about 1 cm/½ in larger than the tops of the moulds. An easy way to do this is to cut out squares of paper larger than the diameter of the moulds. Fold them in half diagonally, then fold the resulting triangle in half. Trim the corners which will produce paper circles when they are unfolded.

Heat the oven to cool (150°C, 300°F, gas 2). Put the sugar lumps and water in a small saucepan and heat gently, stirring until the sugar dissolves. Bring to the boil and boil, stirring constantly, until the resulting syrup is golden brown. Remove the pan from the heat and pour the caramel into the moulds. It becomes hard very quickly so it is important to do this as fast as possible. Pour hot water into the pan so that it will be easier to wash later.

Pour the milk and cream into a heavy saucepan. Split open the vanilla pod lengthways and scrape out the seeds and pulp with a sharp knife. Place the seeds, pulp and pod in the pan with the milk and heat until the milk has almost reached boiling point. Remove the pan from the heat and strain to discard the vanilla pod.

Whisk the eggs and egg yolks together. Gradually add the salt and sugar, whisking constantly. As soon as the mixture becomes very frothy, pour in the hot milk mixture in a thin stream, beating constantly. Then leave to stand for 10 minutes. Skim the foam from the top of the custard using a spoon or ladle (this will prevent bubbles forming later). Pour the custard into the moulds. Grease one side of the paper lids with butter and place them, buttered side down, on the moulds. Press the edges down firmly and tie on with string, if necessary.

Place a thick layer of greaseproof paper on the bottom of a baking tin and stand the moulds on it. Pour enough boiling water into the tin from the side to come halfway up the sides of the moulds. Place in the heated oven immediately and bake for about 1 hour.

Remove the moulds from the tin and allow to cool, then chill for at least 4 hours. To serve, turn out on to individual serving plates.

Our tip

Do not bake the moulds without placing a layer of paper in the baking tin. This protects the caramel from too strong a heat which might result in bubbles appearing in the caramel later. Other paper or cardboard can be used instead of greaseproof paper.

1 **Making the caramel.** Dissolve the sugar lumps in the water in a small saucepan and bring to the boil. Boil, stirring constantly, until the syrup is golden.

2 **Pouring the caramel into the moulds.** Remove the pan from the heat and pour the caramel into the moulds immediately, otherwise it will begin to harden.

3 **Skimming off the foam.** Skim the foam from the surface of the custard with a spoon or ladle, to prevent bubbles forming later. Pour the custard into the moulds.

4 **Covering the moulds.** Place the greaseproof paper lids, buttered side down, on the moulds and press the edges down firmly. Tie with string, if necessary.

Profiteroles with Raspberry Sauce

Light-as-air profiteroles filled with cream and covered with raspberry sauce can be served as dessert or for afternoon tea.

---

100 g/4 oz plain flour
120 ml/4 fl oz water
pinch salt
40 g/1½ oz butter
2–3 eggs (depending on size)
butter and flour for
baking sheet
350 g/12 oz fresh or
frozen raspberries
40 g/1½ oz caster sugar
1 teaspoon lemon juice
2 tablespoons framboise
(raspberry eau-de-vie) or brandy
350 ml/12 fl oz whipping cream
1½ tablespoons vanilla sugar

To cool: 1½ hours
Preparation time: 1 hour

Heat the oven to hot (220°C, 425°F, gas 7). Sift the flour on to a sheet of greaseproof paper. Place the water, salt and butter in a saucepan and heat until the butter has melted and the mixture begins to boil rapidly. Remove from the heat and pour the flour all at once into the still boiling liquid. Quickly stir the mixture together with a wooden spoon, then place the saucepan back on the heat. Continue to stir vigorously until the mixture is thoroughly combined and a white skin begins to form on the bottom of the pan. Remove from the heat, transfer to a bowl and beat in one egg. Leave the paste to cool. When it is lukewarm, beat in a second egg. Take a little of the paste on the end of the wooden spoon and hold it over the bowl. It should be shiny and smooth and hang from the spoon like long icicles. If it does not, add the remaining egg – or half an egg – and beat it into the paste thoroughly. (If very large eggs are used, it may be possible to do without the third egg.) Stop beating as soon as a pliable consistency is obtained; if the paste becomes too soft it will not rise as much as it should.

Grease a baking sheet with butter and dust it with flour. To form the profiteroles, place the paste in a piping bag fitted with a star-shaped tube. Hold the bag directly over the baking sheet and press out small high mounds about the size of a walnut. Leave a good deal of space between the mounds so that they can spread.

Place the baking sheet at once in the heated oven and bake the profiteroles for about 20 minutes. Do not open the oven door during the first 10–15 minutes of cooking or the profiteroles will collapse. Remove the baking sheet from the oven. Slit open the profiteroles with a pair of kitchen scissors or the tip of a sharp knife. This will allow the steam trapped inside to escape. Place on a wire rack to cool.

Meanwhile, make the raspberry sauce. Place the raspberries in a bowl with the caster sugar, lemon juice and half the eau-de-vie or brandy. If using frozen raspberries, leave them to thaw. Mix the ingredients together. Place a sieve over a saucepan and press the fruit mixture through it using the back of a spoon to rub it through. Bring the purée to the boil, stirring all the time, and simmer until the mixture has reduced to a syrupy consistency. Remove from the heat. Leave it to cool, then add the rest of the eau-de-vie to taste.

Whip the cream until it is stiff and sweeten it with the vanilla sugar. Place in a piping bag fitted with the star-shaped tube and fill the profiteroles. Pour the raspberry sauce over them and serve immediately so that they cannot become soft.

1 **Combining the mixture.** Stir vigorously over heat until the flour is combined with the melted mixture. Transfer the paste to a bowl and beat in the eggs one at a time.

2 **Testing the paste.** Take some of the paste on the end of the wooden spoon and hold it over the bowl. It should be smooth and shiny and hang from the spoon like icicles.

3 **Forming the profiteroles.** Hold the piping bag over the baking sheet and press out small mounds the size of a walnut. Leave enough space between them. Place in the oven.

4 **Making the sauce.** Press the raspberries through a fine sieve placed over a saucepan, using the back of a spoon. Simmer until the sauce is syrupy.

Charlotte Royale

Charlotte royale is certainly not one of the quickest of desserts to prepare, but it is surely one of the most delicious.

Serves 8

For the Swiss roll:
butter for greasing tin · 4 eggs
3 tablespoons cold water
75 g/3 oz caster sugar
1 lemon · pinch salt
115 g/4½ oz flour
sugar for sprinkling
1 jar (about 450 g/1 lb)
redcurrant jelly

For the wine cream:
15 g/½ oz powdered gelatine
3 tablespoons water · 3 eggs
75 g/3 oz caster sugar
250 ml/8 fl oz full-bodied
dry white wine
2 tablespoons brandy · pinch salt
300 ml/½ pint whipping cream

Preparation time: 1 hour
To chill: 5–6 hours

Heat the oven to moderately hot (200°C, 400°F, gas 6). Line a 30 × 20 cm (12 × 8 in) Swiss roll tin with greaseproof paper that has been greased with butter.

Separate the eggs into two bowls: the whites into a large one and the yolks in a smaller one. Beat the egg yolks with the water until they are frothy, then gradually beat in 50 g/2 oz of the sugar. Beat until the mixture is white and frothy. If not using an electric mixer, do this in a heatproof bowl over a pan of simmering water. Remove from the water and continue beating until cool.

Rinse the lemon under hot water and pat it dry. Grate off the yellow rind from one half very finely, taking care not to grate the bitter white pith. Set the other half of the lemon aside.

Beat the egg whites with the salt to stiff peaks in the other bowl. Add the remaining sugar, beating constantly. Spoon the egg whites on to the surface of the egg yolk mixture. Sift the flour over the top, sprinkle over the grated lemon rind and fold all together gently. Spread the cake

mixture in the prepared tin. Place on the middle shelf of the heated oven and bake for about 12 minutes.

Meanwhile, spread a clean tea towel on the work surface and sprinkle it generously with sugar. Stir the redcurrant jelly until it is smooth, heating it slightly if necessary.

Turn out the sponge on to the towel. Brush the greaseproof paper with cold water, then peel it off the sponge carefully. Brush the redcurrant jelly over the sponge immediately, leaving a clear border of 1 cm/½ in on all sides. Roll up the sponge from a long side, lifting the edges of the towel to help roll. Leave to cool.

To make the wine cream filling,

sprinkle the gelatine over the water in a small cup and leave to soak for 5 minutes. Grate the rind finely from the reserved half of lemon and squeeze out the juice. Separate the eggs. Beat the egg yolks until they are frothy and add the sugar and wine gradually. Add the lemon rind and juice and the brandy. Place the cup containing the gelatine mixture in a pan of simmering water and stir until the gelatine has dissolved. Stir in 3 tablespoons of the wine mixture, then add to the remaining wine mixture and combine thoroughly. Chill until the mixture has thickened to the consistency of unbeaten egg whites. Beat the egg whites with the salt to stiff peaks. Whip the cream in

another bowl until it is thick. Fold the cream thoroughly into the wine mixture, then gently fold in the egg whites.

Cut the Swiss roll into slices about 8 mm/ in thick. Carefully line a deep round-bottomed bowl or mould that has a 2 litre/3½ pint capacity with the cake slices, pressing them gently together so that they cannot fall off. Wrap any leftover cake slices in cling film or foil and serve on another occasion. Pour in the wine cream.

Chill for 4–5 hours or until the cream is set, then turn out on to a serving dish and serve immediately. The charlotte is best served cut in slices like a fruit pie or cake.

1 **Rolling up the sponge.** Lift the edges of the tea towel and roll up the warm sponge from a long side. Leave the towel over the Swiss roll to prevent it from unrolling, and allow to cool.

2 **Mixing the gelatine** with the wine and egg mixture. When the gelatine is dissolved, add 3 tablespoons of the wine and egg mixture and stir until they are combined.

3 **Filling the mould.** Line the bottom and sides of a deep round-bottomed bowl or mould with Swiss roll slices and then pour in the wine cream. Chill until set.

Tarte aux Poires

Try making this excellent example of a French fruit tart – juicy and tasting strongly of butter.

For the pastry:
225 g/8 oz plain flour
1 small egg
pinch salt
100 g/4 oz sugar
100 g/4 oz cold butter
1 lemon

For the filling:
1.25 kg/2½ lb William pears
juice 1 lemon
40 g/1½ oz butter
65 g/2½ oz sugar
4 tablespoons dry white wine
1 tablespoon amaretto
(almond liqueur)
25 g/1 oz ground almonds
25 g/1 oz fine fresh breadcrumbs
40 g/1½ oz blanched almonds
25 g/1 oz icing sugar

Preparation time: 1 hour
To cool: 30 minutes

First make the pastry. Sift the flour on to a work surface and make a well in the centre. Add the egg and salt to the well and sprinkle the sugar over the egg. Cut the butter into small pieces and place all round the edges of the flour. Rinse the lemon under hot water, dry it thoroughly and grate the rind over the other ingredients. Knead the ingredients together to form a smooth dough, using your fingertips. Knead as quickly as possible so that the ingredients, particularly the butter, do not become warm. If they do, the resulting pastry may be heavy. Roll the dough into a ball, wrap in foil and place it in the refrigerator to rest for 30 minutes.

Meanwhile, prepare the filling. Peel and core the pears and cut lengthways into thin, even-sized slices. Sprinkle the slices with lemon juice to prevent them from going brown. Heat the butter in a saucepan and add the pears, sugar, white wine and almond liqueur. Cover the pan and bring slowly to the boil, shaking the pan frequently. As soon as the mixture begins to boil, reduce the temperature and remove the lid from the pan. Cook, shaking the pan frequently, until the pears are glassy in appearance and the liquid has evaporated. Put aside to cool.

Heat the oven to moderately hot (200°C, 400°F, gas 6). Remove the dough from the refrigerator and roll it out into a round on a floured surface. The dough should be about 3 mm/⅛ in thick. Roll the dough loosely round the rolling pin and unroll it over a 23-cm/9-in flan dish. Press it into the dish and trim the edges with a knife. Any excess dough can be distributed over the bottom of the case; smooth it on to the rest of the dough with the fingers. Prick the dough with a fork so that no bubbles form while it is baking.

Mix the ground almonds with the breadcrumbs and spread evenly over the bottom of the pastry case. Place the cooled pears on top. Slice the blanched almonds and sprinkle over the top. Place on the middle shelf of the heated oven and bake for 25–30 minutes.

Remove the tart from the oven and sift a thick layer of icing sugar over the surface while it is still very hot. Let it cool, and serve lukewarm or cold.

1 **Mixing the dough.** Cut the butter into small pieces and place around the edges of the flour. Grate over the lemon rind. Rub into the flour with the egg and sugar.

2 **Kneading the dough.** Take the dough between your two outstretched palms and press it firmly. Do this as quickly as possible to prevent the dough becoming warm.

3 **Lining the flan dish.** Roll the dough loosely round the rolling pin and roll it out over the flan dish. Press it gently into place with your fingers and trim the edges.

4 **Filling the pastry case.** Sprinkle the breadcrumbs and ground almonds evenly over the bottom of the pastry case. Cover with the cooled pears and sprinkle with sliced almonds.

Salzburg Dumplings

Salzburg dumplings are as much a distinctive feature of Austria as the Prater pleasure park with its big wheel in Vienna. They are not, of course, dumplings of the usual kind, but are a sweet soufflé traditionally baked in three mounds in an oval dish.

½ lemon
4 eggs
pinch salt
25 g/1 oz caster sugar
15 g/½ oz vanilla sugar
15 g/½ oz plain flour
15 g/½ oz butter
icing sugar

Preparation time: 30 minutes

Heat the oven to moderately hot (200°C, 400°F, gas 6). Rinse the lemon under hot water and pat it dry. Grate off the yellow rind very finely, taking care not to grate the bitter-tasting white pith.

Separate the eggs into two bowls: the whites into a large one and the yolks into a small one. Separate each egg very carefully; there should not be even the slightest bit of yolk in the whites. Add the salt to the egg whites and whisk them until they are stiff; they will be ready when it is possible to cut into them with a knife or the blades of the whisk and the impression is still there a few seconds later. Mix the caster sugar with the vanilla sugar and let it trickle into the egg whites, whisking all the time. Sprinkle the lemon rind over the top and fold in gently.

Beat the egg yolks until they are pale and creamy. Add 2 tablespoons of the meringue to the egg yolks and mix together well. Let the yolks glide on to the surface of the remaining meringue. Do not fold in. Sift the flour over the top, and fold the mixture together very gently but thoroughly with a spatula; do not stir or the mixture will lose some of its lightness.

Heat the butter in an oval gratin dish until it starts to bubble. It should not become brown. Using two tablespoons, lift one-third of the mixture at a time into the dish so that the three mounds (or dumplings) are next to one another. Place on the middle shelf of the heated oven

immediately and bake for about 5 minutes, then reduce the temperature to very cool (110°C, 225°F, gas ¼) and bake for a further 10 minutes or until the tops are light brown; the dumplings should still be creamy and soft inside.

Remove from the oven and dredge with sifted icing sugar. Serve immediately since the dumplings will collapse at the slightest draught or if they have to wait. It is better to ask your guests to wait for the dumplings rather than the other way round!

1 **Adding the egg yolks to the meringue.** Beat the egg yolks in a second bowl and add 2 tablespoons of the meringue mixture. Mix well before letting the yolks glide on to the remaining meringue.

2 **Adding the flour.** Sift the flour over the top of the meringue and egg yolk mixtures. Fold together gently but thoroughly using a spatula. Do not stir or the mixture will lose some of its lightness.

3 **Placing the dumpling mixture in the dish.** Heat the butter in the dish. Remove one-third of the mixture at a time with two tablespoons and place in three mounds in the dish.

Pashka

The decoration of pashka should be as rich as the ingredients because it is a special Easter dish in Russia, and in Europe a delight for the gourmet.

Serves 8

---

100 g/4 oz unblanched almonds
150 g/5 oz butter
800 g/1¾ lb quark, or
other low-fat soft or
cottage cheese
3 egg yolks
100 g/4 oz caster sugar
6 tablespoons double cream
50 g/2 oz raisins
25 g/1 oz glacé cherries
40 g/1½ oz candied lemon peel
40 g/1½ oz candied orange peel
1–2 vanilla pods
100 g/4 oz mixed candied
fruit for decoration

Preparation time: 1¼ hours
To chill: 12–24 hours

Pashka is as much a part of the Russian Easter as painted eggs and vodka. Each family naturally has its own recipe but the pashka is always richly decorated and made in a special pyramid-shaped wooden form, perforated all round and lined with muslin through which the excess liquid can drain. As such moulds are unobtainable here, we suggest the use of a new clay flower pot with a diameter of about 15 cm/6 in; this can be lined with a rectangular piece of muslin measuring 80 × 100 cm/36 × 40 in.

Place the almonds in a bowl and pour boiling water over them. Leave to blanch for 3–5 minutes, then drain and rub off the skins between your fingers. Spread the nuts out on a clean tea towel and leave them to dry.

Cream the butter in a mixing bowl until softened. Gradually add the quark or other cheese, beating it well so that the mixture becomes light and frothy. Set aside.

Beat the egg yolks in a heatproof bowl and add the sugar. Place the bowl over a pan of hot but not boiling water and whisk together. Gradually whisk in the cream. Continue to whisk until the mixture becomes thick and creamy. Do not let it become too hot or the egg yolks will curdle. Remove the bowl from the hot water and stand it in a bowl of cold water. Leave it to cool, beating vigorously from time to time.

Meanwhile, rinse the raisins in hot water and rub dry in a tea towel. Chop the glacé cherries coarsely or cut into quarters. Finely chop the candied lemon and orange peels. Set aside one-third of the blanched almonds for the decoration, and finely chop the remainder. Mix the chopped almonds with the raisins, cherries, lemon peel and orange peel. Cut the vanilla pods open right down their length and scrape out the pulp and seeds with a knife.

Pour the egg yolk and cream mixture into the butter and cheese mixture, followed by the mixed nuts and fruits and the vanilla pulp and seeds. Mix everything together lightly but thoroughly.

Rinse the flower pot well in hot water. Fold the piece of muslin together two or three times and dampen it. Use it to line the flower pot, leaving a border of about 5 cm/2 in hanging over the rim all the way round. Stand a wire rack (or a cork cut into three equally thick slices) on a large soup plate and place the lined flower pot on top, making sure the hole in the bottom of the pot is not blocked up. Balance the mixing bowl on the rim of the lined flower pot so that it holds the muslin in place and pour in the mixture. Fold the edges of the damp muslin over the mixture all round and press down firmly.

First put a plate that exactly fits the flower pot on top of the mixture, then stand a pot on this and fill it with water. Allow the pashka to firm up and dry out slightly in the refrigerator.

Before serving unfold the muslin cloth, place a large plate on top of the pashka and turn it out of its mould, as you would a cake. Remove the flower pot and peel off the muslin. Decorate the pashka generously with the candied fruits and reserved whole blanched almonds.

1 Pouring in the mixture. Balance the mixing bowl on the rim of the lined flower pot so that it holds the muslin lining in place, then pour in the mixture.

2 Sealing the pashka. Fold the overhanging muslin up over the mixture all round the flower pot and press it down firmly. Press carefully so the flower pot does not tip over.

3 Weighting the pashka. Select a plate that will just fit inside the top of the flower pot and place it on the mixture. Weight with a pot filled with water.

Glossary of Cooking Terms

Al dente of pasta, firm to the bite

Allumettes vegetables cut into matchstick-sized pieces

Antipasti cold or hot Italian hors d'oeuvre

A point referring to meat, medium cooked

Aspic a clear jelly made from the cooked, clarified juices of meat, chicken or fish

Bain marie or water bath, a large pan filled with hot water in which delicate dishes can be cooked, or kept warm

Baking blind baking pastry cases without a filling. To help keep their shape they are first lined with greaseproof paper or foil and filled with dried beans, peas or bread crusts

Barding covering lean meat, game or poultry with strips of fat to prevent the flesh drying out during cooking

Blanching to boil briefly in order to: set the colour of food prior to freezing, or cooking by another method; loosen the skins of fruits or nuts to make peeling easier; remove unpleasant flavours and impurities

Boning a bunch or muslin bag, of herbs and seasonings, often composed of sprigs of parsley, thyme, marjoram and bay, with a clove of garlic and black peppercorns

Braising Browning in hot fat, then simmering in a covered pan with vegetables and a seasoned liquid

Brine a salted water solution used for pickling and preserving

Brioche a rich yeast pastry or bread, slightly sweetened

Brûlé a term used to describe sweet dishes, such as custards, finished with a caramelised sugar glaze

Cannelloni pasta tubes, stuffed with a savoury filling

Charlotte a hot pudding, consisting of a bread-lined mould filled with fruit; or a cold dessert, again using a mould (called a charlotte mould), this time lined with sponge fingers and filled with fruit and/or cream

Chantilly lightly sweetened whipped cream

Chaud-froid a formal, classic presentation made from meat, poultry, game or fish covered with a creamy sauce; often, too, coated with aspic and highly decorated

Chiffonade a garnish of shredded lettuce, sorrel or spinach, used to decorate doups or cold dishes

Clarifying 'clearing' butter or fats by heating, allowing to cool and settling then filtering; or clearing stock with beaten egg white, to make consommé

Cocotte small, ovenproof, porcelain or earthenware cooking dish, in which individual portions can be both cooked and served

Compote dessert of fresh or dried fruit, poached in syrup

Consommé a clear meat or fish stock, made as for ordinary stock, then clarified with beaten egg white

Court bouillon highly seasoned liquid in which fish are poached

Crêpe a thin, egg pancake, sweet or savoury

Custard a creamy sauce or base for a dessert made by cooking together egg yolks and milk or cream

Dariole small, smooth-sided moulds used for making sweet and savoury creams

Daube a stew of braised meat and vegetables

Deep-frying cooking in deep, hot fat

Deglazing adding stock or wine to pan juices and briefly cooking together to make a sauce

Demi-glace A concentrated, rich brown gravy or sauce base

Dice to cut into small cubes

Dredging dusting or sprinkling food with flour or sugar

Dressing a sauce for a salad; or trussing poultry or boned meat with string to hold its shape when cooking

Dumpling a small, savoury ball, often made from a stuffing or potato mixture; or a fruit-filled dough-based pudding

En papillote food wrapped and cooked in buttered greaseproof paper or foil parcels

Entrée a warm or cold dish served as part of a formal meal, where it follows the fish course and precedes the main course

Farce a filling for pies, terrines, meats, poultry, fish or vegetables, usually consisting of finely chopped or puréed meat, fish or vegetables, seasoned

Ficeler	to tie up with string
Fines herbes	finely chopped herbs, used in various combinations, but often consisting of parsley, chervil, tarragon and chives
Flambé	food tossed, i.e. 'flamed', in a pan to which burning brandy or other spirit has been added
Fleurons	small, half-moon-shaped puff pastries used to garnish savory dishes and soups
Folding in	incorporating one ingredient into another, using a metal spoon or a spatula
Fond blanc	white veal or chicken stock
Fond de gibier	game stock
Fond de volaille	white poultry stock
Fricassée	a white stew, generally of veal, lamb or chicken cooked in stock and finished with cream and egg yolks
Fumet	a concentrated stock generally made from fish, but also from meat or vegetables
Galantine	a cold dish of boned and stuffed poultry, game or meat, generally glazed with aspic
Garnish	an edible decoration for a savoury dish
Gelatine	a pure, tasteless bone extract in powder or leaf form which melts in hot liquid and forms a jelly when cold
Glace de viande	a highly reduced meat stock of veal, chicken, game or fish, used to improve sauces or glaze meats
Glaze	a glossy finish given to food by brushing with beaten egg (before cooking) or sweet syrup (after cooking)
Gratiner	to brown under the grill to produce a crust
Gravy	a sauce made by boiling roasted meat or poultry juices with stock and/or wine, sometimes thickened with a little flour
Hors d'oeuvre	a hot or cold appetiser or first course
Infusing	steeping ingredients in liquid to extract their flavour
Jugged	meat, for example jugged hare, stewed in a covered pot
Julienne	fine strips of vegetable or truffle, included in or accompanying a dish
Jus	pure meat juice or roasting juices, used as a gravy
Lard	pork fat. *To lard*, to insert strips of pork fat into lean meat to keep it moist during cooking
Lardon	a small strip of pork fat
Lier	to thicken
Macerate	to soak a food in flavoured liquid, to soften it
Marinade	a blend of oil, spices, herbs and other flavourings used to tenderise and flavour meat, game or fish
Mie de pain	white bread crumbs without crust
Mijoter	to simmer or braise over very low heat
Mirepoix	finely diced root vegetables, onion and bacon lightly fried in butter and used as a base for brown sauces and stews
Monter	to beat butter into a sauce or soup
Mousse	light sweet or savoury cold dish made with cream, whipped egg white, and gelatine
Nap	to mask, or cover, foods with jelly or sauce
Navarin	a stew of lamb and vegetables
Panada	a binding or thickening agent made of flour or bread
Paner	to dip first in flour, then in breadcrumbs
Pâté	savoury mixture, baked, either in a terrine or a pastry case, then served cold
Pâté feuilletée	puff pastry
Pickling	preserving vegetables or fruit in brine or a vinegar solution
Poach	to cook slowly without allowing to boil
Primeurs	early or spring vegetables, early fruit, or young wine
Purée	sieved raw or cooked food
Quenelle	a light, small savoury dumpling made of meat or fish, served as a garnish or in a delicate sauce
Ragoût	a stew of chopped meat and vegetables
Reduce	to boil liquid such as stock, soup or sauce to thicken or concentrate it and enhance the flavour
Refresh	to cool boiled vegetables or meat under cold running water
Remoulade	highly seasoned mayonnaise with chopped herbs, anchovy fillets, capers and gherkins
Rissole	fried or baked until brown and crisp
Roasting	cooking in the oven, on a spit or over an open fire
Roux	a blend of melted butter and flour, lightly cooked together and used as a base for savoury sauces
Salmi	a stew made from roasted game
Sauter	to quickly fry food in shallow oil
Savarin	rich yeast cake, baked in a ring mould and then soaked in liqueur-flavoured syrup
Skimming	removing scum from the surface of stock or broth
Soufflé	sweet or savoury baked dish based on a sauce or purée, enriched with egg yolks, into which the beaten whites are then folded
Steaming	cooking in water without the food coming into contact with the liquid

Stewing	simmering food gently in a covered pan
Straining	separating liquids from solids by passing them through a sieve or through muslin
Stuff	to fill with a seasoned mixture (stuffing)
Terrine	an earthenware pot for cooking and serving pâté
Trussing	tying a joint of meat or a bird into a compact shape with skewers, string, or both, before cooking
Vanilla sugar	castor sugar flavoured with vanilla pods
Velouté	basic white sauce made from a *roux* base and veal, chicken or fish stock
Vinaigrette	an emulsion of oil, vinegar and seasonings generally used as a salad dressing
Vol-au-vent	light, puff pastry case
Zest	the outer skin or rind of citrus fruits, often grated or peeled to flavour sweet sauces and desserts

Index